Erotic Body Prayer

Pathways to Pray Through the Body and Build Ecstatic Community

Drawing by Rev. Dr. Dan Newman

Kirk Prine, Ed.D.

Dr. Kirk Prine, CMT
4621 18th Street
San Francisco, CA 94114
www.fleshandspirit.org

Cover art by Rev. Dan Newman, Ph.D., design by Allen Siewert

ISBN 978-1-4303-0107-3

Erotic Body

Prayer

Greg,
The joy of sharing
this adventure with
you fills my heart.
Live fully in the
awakening! ♡
Kirk

Acknowledgements

The ease of this book comes with gratitude first to my husband, Donny Lobree, whose spiritual encouragement and quick typing skills offered a joyful space to write this revision. Our own journey of ecstasy is an important aspect to the story being told. Also to my fellow ecstatic practitioner, Reed Waller, I offer sincerest appreciation for editing this narrative with such care.

I also wish to extend gratitude to all along the way who have influenced my ecstatic path. Thank you to my parents Laurel and Anna Prine who nurtured me in a folk spirituality that acknowledges the spirits of ancestors and the possibility of life beyond the visible universe.

Oddly enough, I give thanks for those Charismatic Christian leaders who opened a doorway for me to experience the ecstatic spirit that I now know in ever expanding ways.

To those who are my primary teachers—Dr. Don Clark who has been a mentor; Sri Ronji (Ron Roth) who has demonstrated the power of spirit in a progressive spirituality; Shankari, The Spiritual Alchemist; Rev. Dr. Jim Mitulski and Rev. Dr. Penny Nixon, two queer prophetic voices of our time—I offer profound gratitude.

To the pioneers and colleagues of body wisdom: James Broughton, Joseph Kramer, Collin Brown, Sequoia Thom Lundy and Andrew Ramer, thank you for your work that encouraged me on the journey of integration.

Thank you to those who played a significant role in my development: Dr. Tom Kalin, sex therapist, who supervised my therapeutic skills; my educators of spirit, who may have only

touched me briefly through workshops or consultations, peo-
ple like Peter Bear Walks, Maladoma Patrice Somé, Dr. Dolores
Kreiger, Carolyn Myss, Dr. Elizabeth Kübler Ross, Dr. Donald
Pachuta, Dr. Charles Steinberg, Dr. Candice Pert, Dr. Joanne
Loulan and Dr. Charles Whitfield, all of whom influenced my
understanding of mind, body and spirit.

I would also like to recognize all the men who have been in
Flesh and Spirit Community as members, leaders, staff and
board. This journal is your story through my experience.
Thank you for generously showing up to build this adventurous
new consciousness.

Finally, to Spirit and the energies that offer me guidance,
the ancestors, peaceful warriors, lovers, sacred prostitutes, elders, mystics and prophets who paved the way for Queer people
to share in bringing enlightenment.
Thank you.

"If you ask me how
Jesus raised the dead,
Kiss me on the lips."

Rumi

Contents

Preface

The first version of this book began as the *Erotic Body Prayer Manual* which was a joint collaboration of Kirk Prine and Terry Huwe. The focus of the manual was primarily Queer men interested either in Flesh and Spirit Community or activity pursuing an erotic spiritual journey. The contributions of Terry Huwe in editing and shaping some of the initial manual allowed it to be released in a timely fashion for basic instructional needs. I offer much appreciation to Terry for helping launch the first edition which laid the groundwork for this book.

Along with many spiritual traditions, this work draws from a social, political, psychological and theoretical base that affirms the divinity of all people and their right to inclusion. Queer Theory, congruence theory, feminist theory and attributional theory are present in both the language and content of Erotic Body Prayer: Pathways to Praying through the Body and Build Ecstatic Community.

The language of gender, the pronouns "he/she", or "him/her", are used when speaking of all persons. People who are Transgendered female-to-male (FTM) are part of Flesh and Spirit Community and are spoken of as men who love men or brothers. This language feels appropriate to these members. Since much of this book is designed to awaken Queer men on their path of ecstasy and is specific at times to Flesh and Spirit Community members, "he/him" is used intentionally.

"Queer" is also used as an academic term and as a politically inclusive term of gay, lesbian, bisexual, Transgendered (both FTM and male-to-female) and those who identify as multigender. "Queer" is often used in this text as an inclusive adjective, i.e., "Queer Men" to describe gay, bisexual and transgendered men who love men. In addition, the word "Queer" will be capitalized to emphasize our tribal nature.

Reclaiming words, especially used by those who have oppressed Queer people, is advocated not as a political agenda alone, but a spiritual tool of empowerment that reconnects us with the ideas and energies of compassionate power. Prayer, body, erotic, sex, God/Goddess, sacred prostitute, Christian, Muslim and witch are just a few words worth taking back as we experience their power, beauty and consciousness.

A word that the erotic spirituality movement has reclaimed is "ecstasy." While the common connotation in our culture is of an intense pleasure, one of its definitions is "a state of overwhelming emotion."[1] Those who have experienced ecstatic trance through ritual, bodywork, or erotic energy work know that the ecstatic state creates a union with the Whole, with all that is Holy, that encompasses the range of all emotion, from rapturous joy to cathartic grief, while still including intense pleasure. It is essential to understanding the work of Erotic Body Prayer that we grasp this more comprehensive definition of ecstasy.

The use of language holds intention and energetic power. Thus, such attention to words is not just an attempt to be politically correct, but to equalize power for all as a spiritual action. Even in this book, language may be incomplete or may sustain old models that no longer serve a new consciousness. It is my desire that we grow together in words which vibrate and create the truth that frees all.

One of those incomplete words in this narrative is the word

"my." "My" is intended to denote a personal relationship with a person, place or thing in these writings, not to infer possession. I believe we are all magicians in influencing and creating our world. I do not believe we ultimately possess anything.

As with any material I teach, one does not need to entirely understand all the experiences and frameworks described in these writings for them to be of value. Use your language of comprehension. Let this narrative challenge you out of your comfort zone while maintaining your own integrity, meaning or metaphor to guide you a bit further on the ecstatic journey.

This book is filled with names and stories of Queer people. With exception to a fundamentalist minister mentioned in this book, all of the persons think, act or challenge the world for love in ways that categorize them loosely as Queer. That being said, not all persons acknowledged in this book are Queer by sexual orientation. However, all persons represented do think outside the box.

Read this book to open up Queer conversations about our world. Read this book with the words of Jean Houston as a context:

"The world is too complex for linear

analytic thinking now. To be smart in the

global village means thinking with your

stomach, thinking rhythmically, thinking

organically, thinking in terms of yourself as

an interwoven piece of nature." [1]

The Phoenix Rising

This new edition of *Erotic Body Prayer: Pathways to Pray Through the Body and Build Ecstatic Community* takes on a broader conversation of the ecstatic path for Queer men on a spiritual journey. It may also appeal to the broader community inclusive of genders and sexual orientations. Thus, this work intends to offer a framework for Queer men choosing to participate in Flesh and Spirit Community while opening a broader dialogue about consciousness in this evolving new world.

Using my own personal journey as the thread to weave this tapestry together, I have structured this work as a compilation of ancient and contemporary wisdom combined with science and spirituality.

This broader revision comes as a result of the developmental nature of building, nurturing and sustaining a progressive Queer men's erotic spiritual community, Flesh and Spirit, as well as the initiations I experienced through a series of life-changing events.

The Fire

It has been a year since that incredible morning. My vantage point now has been altered (as one might expect) through the lenses of time, space and miraculous events following the morning of the fire.

981 Haight

My partner, Donny, and I were doing our usual dating rituals for that day. We got up from his home where I slept that night to take him to his 6 am yoga class. After dropping him off, I drove one block away to my house on Haight St. in San Francisco. My home, a rented Victorian with a long Queer history, was the primary meeting place for Flesh and Spirit Community. For years, most of our workshops exploring The Peaceful Warrior, The Lover, The Sacred Prostitute, and The Elder were held there. Monthly we met there for prayer rituals, drumming circles, Reiki clinics and ecstatic massage. This house had also been a Queer space where James

Broughton, Harry Hay and numcruos other Queer leaders, healers, sexual healers, activists and thinkers had conjured many a spell of change upon themselves and the world. 981 Haight St seemed to hold the energy of Queer histories. It was like stepping into a temple steeped in ritual meditation. My experience of this house, especially during our monthly drumming circles, was a vivid sense of the ancestors vibrating through the walls.

As I pulled up to the driveway, I immediately noticed a huge pile of debris in front of the house. I seldom cuss, but I remember throwing up my judging statement, "Damn my neighbors," thinking they had thrown their garbage in my driveway again. Then, to my shock, I realized the house itself was the debris.

A numbing disbelief followed as I met the firefighters who had been there since midnight putting out the residual fire that had consumed the house. Running to get my partner from his yoga class, I returned with him to walk through the remaining framework of this 3-story charred building.

I cried as he held me and quickly said "thank you" to the house for caring for me/us. Even in those early moments, the magnitude of my past and future seemed to rush through my body. A gateway had opened unbeknownst to my conscious planning. We left the house, releasing its energies for the first of what would be many times.

The research on peak experiences speaks of intense feelings that we judge as either positive or negative. These feelings become deeply locked into our memory banks As I walked away from the house that day I knew doors yet to be revealed had been opened. As I had taught in workshops for years, it was now my choice to decide how I wished to hold this experience and it would be from these perceptions that I would create my next reality.

A phrase from the Christian Testament Lord's Prayer is "Hallowed be thy Name." In one translation from the Aramaic, the language Jesus spoke, "hallowed"[3], means to "sweep out" "make room for" or "soften the ground" The witches of the twelfth to fifteenth centuries would perform a ritual of sweeping a path in preparation for a new spell or new creation to come forth. Another meaning for "hallowed" is "Oh Thou! The Breathing Life of all." Since the day of the fire and each subsequent day thereafter, I have felt my heart has been swept out, freed of attachments to make room for some new Breath of Life.

The day of the fire was just three days before Flesh and Spirit Community's retreat entitled *Ecstatic Gatekeepers: Conversation with our Ancestors*. That very evening after the fire, Flesh and Spirit Community was to meet for a ritual in preparation for the retreat. The ritual would involve blessing candles (in glass containers) that each man would light while on the retreat or, if he was not attending, light in solidarity with us from his home.

Most of what one calls "possessions" were destroyed in the fire. Only about five small boxes of things were salvaged. One of the amazing things saved was a cardboard box containing the forty candles to be used in the blessing which sat in our primary meeting space. Everything around the box was incinerated by the fire, yet the candles remained.

We all met that night in my partner's home sharing tears, stories and initial gifts as we blessed our candles. In this developmental process of building a progressive Queer men's erotic spiritual community, not only had I changed, but the community had as well.

Starting Over

When all one's tangible possessions have been destroyed the opportunity presents itself to start over. Starting over for Flesh and Spirit meant we got to restructure and build a new foundation. We thought we knew who we were, but we got to ask the question afresh, "Who are we now?"

Along with the community's redefining itself and exploring its core values, I, too, was plunged into a flow of energy that both excited and frightened me. My work has always felt shamanistic. That day it was clear I had experienced an initiation to the underworld only to rise again like the phoenix. Little did I know what shapes and forms this new creation was to take or embody.

Firstly, Flesh and Spirit Community was without a home. Luckily, interim gifts were almost immediately set in place. Metropolitan Community Church (MCC) opened its doors to allow us to continue some of our workshops in their space. An announcement was made at one of the MCC services and soon a parishioner donated a free space for three months so I could continue my bodywork practice. People seemed to be reaching out with many kinds of support over the first few months. The sense of community seemed launched into a new level.

The journey through grief, fear, excitement and freedom flavored both my personal process as well as the process of the community. Somehow, this experience of initiation had a sense of Divine Right Order.

Prior to the fire, my partner and I had planned to go to London and Prague together. The timing of the retreat and then traveling to Europe to heal and renew seemed perfect.

My heart had been "hallowed," swept; and I knew that space would be filled with something new. The "new" showed up in an extraordinary experience while we were in London. Donny and I made love that morning (probably opening up the circuits for the experience to follow). We were to go out and meet Sue, a friend of his. Sue was, among many things, a healer and a channel. The plan was to meet her at Westminster Abbey for an Evensong service.

Getting up from our bed to ready ourselves to meet Sue, I had the sudden realization I didn't know who I was. I didn't know my name. I didn't know who Donny was or his name. A weird sensation of peace flooded my being and body while an edge of fear laced my cognitive process. I knew I was safe and I knew I was supposed to be with Donny and he was my partner, but beyond that I was a blank slate.

For about two hours I stayed close to Donny, gathering whatever hints I could as we chatted. When we met Sue, she used his name, he used her name and then they used my name. Finally I had something to identify myself with. I have had many ecstatic experiences in my life. In Flesh and Spirit, we regularly created rituals using ecstatic massage, a combination of touch (including erotic stimulation), breathwork, prayerful intention, and sometimes Reiki. In ecstatic massage I always connected with ancestors. In other rituals using breath, sound, elements, touch and movement over the years I experienced the Divine. Through healers, shamans or mystics I have had many extraordinary energetic experiences. Once I meditated and fasted for 13 days and I was taken up into a wave of joy of an intensity that words cannot describe.

Yet, this experience of ecstasy in London was unique. The only clue I had during the two hours of altered consciousness was the concept of "walk-ins" that I had read in a book 20 years prior. (I subsequently remembered that is was Ruth Montgomery's *Strangers Among Us*.) The book describes souls, energies, entities, or personalities that enter the body, something like the concept of reincarnation, but occurring after birth. A walk-in can completely replace the existing personality or soul of that body, but my experience felt more like an opening up to some large spirit rather than an invasive replacement. I felt as though I was connecting to the Divine, and eventually I integrated this opened spiritual connection into my ongoing life.

Somehow it resonated with me that some energy of guidance was coming through in a different way than I had ever known before. I was at ease in the confusing mental sorting out that was going on knowing some wonderful gift was being bestowed. It was truly mystical. The work of the ecstatic path which I have taught for many years to Queer men was about to have broader meanings and implications for my mission of love.

In the subsequent months after the experience in London, I began doing automatic writing allowing this guidance to speak through me. Instead of monitoring the writing, I simply let the writing go wherever it would.

My guidance took on the name Shimakataya. One day, welcoming my guidance, I wrote:

"Relax... You will find a space. It will have a corri-

dor. There will be a front private entrance. There

will be steps going up the side. There will be a

small garden and two flower boxes for you to plant

flowers... Your meeting with Penny

is important."

The deadline to move from the donated space was in one week. None of the leads that brothers from Flesh and Spirit had gathered with me had produced viable locations to do intentional erotic spiritual work. Nevertheless, only hours after writing that affirmation from Shimakataya I met with my dear friend, Penny Nixon. In my writing that morning, Shimakataya also told me my time with Penny would be important. Penny, while checking in with me, mentioned that one of the MCC clergy was moving and a space in the Castro District was opening up. In minutes I met with the property manager and walked through the exact space that had been described in my writing. The entrance, the steps, the garden and flower boxes all were there. A rush of gratitude tingled through my body as the realization of desire for a new space had been manifested. I knew I was cared for in this clear demonstration of spirit.

The gifts or initiations of the fire were numerous: freedom from attachments to material things (both sacred and profane); an opportunity to re-evaluate who I was and who the Flesh and Spirit community was, to build a new foundation that would be true for us in our development; and, of course, the depth of love experienced in founding community and spirit that is unique when facing challenges together.

Initiations produce leaders, teachers, healers and maturity. Flesh and Spirit held a day of visioning facilitated by Elliott Brown. In that process, we created the mission statement and vision statement to speak to who we see ourselves becoming. Here are those statements:

We are a flourishing intentional community of
queer men who bring enlightenment, love, libera-
tion, healing, knowledge, power, and wholeness
around issues of queer men's identity, spirituality,
and sexuality. We are socially progressive, financially solvent, and organizationally stable. We have
the power to bring positive change to the world.
We perceive ourselves as radiant "bringers of
light" to all who experience our work. San
Francisco serves as our home base, but our programs and impact extend around the world. In our
commitment to inclusion, we offer the invitation

to all queer men to experience the gifts of our

community and programs. To the queer and non-

queer communities, we provide gifts of healing

and we raise consciousness. We serve as an exam-

ple of how queer men bring unique gifts to the

greater world."4

In a later visioning session, our brother Greg John encapsulat-
ed our mission thus:

"Touching Skin, Opening Hearts, Raising, Spirits."

This re-vision of the book, Erotic Body Prayer, is a necessary
expression of our developmental process as a progressive Queer
men's erotic spiritual community. May the themes, stories and
processes enclosed here activate principles in you to create your
own heart's desires.

I.
Loving Ideas: Political and Spiritual Archetypes

"Give them hope!"

Harvey Milk

The Earth, the Body Erotic and Spirit

In this first decade of the new millennium post-September 11, 2001, as we face increasing challenges such as disillusionment with the war in Iraq, natural disasters, weather changes and questions of global stability, many seek deeper meaning to their lives. The chasms between ideologies, religions and worldviews often seem more polarized with each day. There is little support for a rich, abundant, integrated life honoring the body and the spirit of all people. At the same time, Queer people and others who live their lives without the full support of society are doubly challenged in their journeys of self-discovery and integration of body, mind and spirit. Despite the challenges, a conscious commitment to integrating all of the aspects of our lives—both physical and spiritual—is well worth the effort. When individuals commit to healing journeys, they not only affect their own lives but also society at large, as well as the natural world that makes society possible.

In the process of healing and self-discovery, some of the most important starting points are experiential and reside within our physical bodies. Integrated, healing journeys that enlist the full power of body and mind require total self-acceptance, including the acceptance of our erotic bodies. Indeed, Queer (Gay, Lesbian and Transgendered) people have a special potential to develop an awareness of the body as a teacher. Long denied outside affirmation for our erotic experience, we began a healing journey by simply coming out and facing the fullness of our desire for same-sex or even polymorphous love.

At the same time, integrated healing work honors both the intellect and the heart. We can grow by linking experiential body-work with the study of shamanic practices and the Queer role in history that the textbooks have overlooked. As King Solomon said, "There is nothing new under the sun."[1] Rediscovery of our ancestors and their lives is fundamental to Queer people. Our key challenge as healers and lovers is to draw together the powerful messages of our ancestors through our own erotic bodies.

Contemporary author Alice Walker affirms the integrity of the open-ended spiritual search for healing. In her book of essays, *Anything We Love Can be Saved*, she says, "All people deserve to worship a God who also worships them," and "Everyone deserves a God who adores our freedom."[2] Walker's ideas about earth and nature naturally speak to Queer people who must listen to their own bodies to connect with Spirit. When we integrate our physical and erotic natures with our urge to build community and political justice for all, power is unleashed to improve the general health of our communities and the fate of the earth.

II. Erotic Body Prayer: The Journey of Healing

Erotic Body Prayer is an accumulation of compassionate and holistic ideas found in Tantra, Wicca, Buddhism, Neo-paganism, Asian Medicine, Judaism, Christianity, Sufism, and the stories of mystics who lived outside any institutional religious structures. Recovering the richness of these traditions, which are not often preserved in official scriptures, is both a challenge and an adventure. Queer people will recognize the essential need to pull together many diverse ideas to build the communities they desire for themselves.

It is vitally important to recognize the Queer tribe as an erotic people, comprising individuals living fully in their bodies and embracing the messages they receive and share in their physical vessels. Eroticism, lovingly and mindfully practiced, is an ecstatic gateway to the divine. Honoring the fullness of our erotic bodies is a vital step on the path of becoming whole. Holding the erotic as sacred is imperative if we are to share our gifts of wisdom and healing with the larger community. If we suppress our erotic spirit we will suffocate our unique gifts of healing, thereby banishing ourselves from the garden of delight and healing our bodies provide for us. Whether our interests are political, professional or spiritual, the work of body-mind integration is a key avenue to self-empowerment.

The Six Archetypes on the Ecstatic Path

Erotic Body Prayer draws great power from archetypal images. Archetypes are most commonly associated with noted psychoanalyst C.G. Jung, but they also have great power to give meaning to our personal stories, helping us create a "narrative" awareness of our own development. It is not necessary to adopt esoteric or academic levels of thinking to understand their power. They can be harnessed and invited as healing guides directly through experiential work that involves the body.

There are six principal archetypes that create the central framework of Erotic Body Prayer. They are archetypes that may apply to anyone on a healing journey. However, they are especially applicable to Queer people, and may empower our political and spiritual journeys. In Erotic Body Prayer practice, each archetype is like a guide that helps us understand our erotic experience, inspiring us to make positive contributions to our partners and communities. The archetypes also work together, defining a path of discovery.

Body Stories

Archetypes tap into our unconscious mind and spirit. They help us see who we are and what our work in this lifetime may be. By reflecting upon the meaning of different symbolic systems that personify the psyche, we can recover greater awareness of our unconscious yearnings and motives. In this respect, working with archetypes is very complimentary to experiential body-oriented work which can awaken memories and feelings we store in the tissues and energetic fields of the body. In 1992, the year Flesh & Spirit Community was founded, I created a term to describe this internally recorded material: "body stories."

Our lives provide many examples of how archetypal knowledge can teach and heal. For example, a friend of mine was severely beaten on the street one day, leaving him in a state of total amnesia. He had no recollection of his prior life whatsoever. Gradually, however, he relearned how to speak but still remained unaware of his past. Friends told him he had been a ballet dancer. Despite having no memory of dancing, he began to take classes to experiment with dance movement. As he attended class, he discovered that his body "remembered" how to move, even though his mind had forgotten (This experience I'll refer to later as an example of a body story).

We need not experience such trauma to know the value of body wisdom. Often the work we choose for ourselves becomes a gateway to the body's library of wisdom. Matthew Simmons,[1] a bodyworker who has worked with the Body Electric School of Massage , has spoken at length about his work as a Sacred Prostitute. In particular, Matthew has developed rituals and skills to help men facing death open themselves more easily to the process. He has called this work "Midwiving the Dying." Matthew had no formal training in this work, yet he knew what to do as he listened to his body. The actions Matthew described were remarkably identical to ancient traditions of sexual healing and bridge-building between our world and the spirit world.

These two examples illustrate how the psyche can be linked to body wisdom thereby creating new power and healing potential. Like many stories of healing, we see wonder and miracles become interjected into ordinary lives. Our healing journeys, even though they may be anecdotal, informal,and lacking in measurable empirical evidence are nonetheless journeys of power. Matthew Simmons has been a channel and guide for many men simply by being available to his own body wisdom, allowing instinct, and a sense of what "feels right" to guide his own ritual work. My traumatized friend single-handedly awakened a beautiful and precious side of himself that had been lost. Each of us can achieve similar breakthroughs as we transform our lives into journeys of integration and healing.

It is commonly accepted that one's parents can pass along the genetic predisposition to diseases and conditions. Perhaps on a genetic level, much as our ancient ancestors suggested. there are generational stories passed on through the body. If this be so, as I describe the concepts and experiences in this book, I would ask you to open to the possibility of breaking this generational pattern. The notion of body stories will contribute to this consideration.

Equally so, possibly all the wisdom of the body to heal to be free and transform the world is also contained in our cellular structure. The following six archetypes (listed below) are particularly useful for this exploration.

The six archetypes I have identified as particularly useful are listed below. There are many archetypes to consider, but these six have special significance to the practice of Erotic Body Prayer. Each archetype depicts a model of ecstasy particularly beneficial to those who identify as Queer or outside convention.

The Peaceful Warrior:
The Guiding Principle to Ecstatic Work

The first archetype is the Peaceful Warrior, which Buddhism defines as one who is willing to know oneself and willing to face one's fears. This archetype seems universal since it can be found in almost all spiritual traditions. Numerous labels have been given to this archetype with meanings similar to the definition from both recent and ancient Buddhism. Spiritual warrior, heartful warrior, rainbow warrior, new warrior and sometimes even just warrior have held the meanings and attributes espoused in this work.

Each of the six major archetypes in this book addresses the integration of some polarity. "Peaceful," a word of inner direction, compassion, mercy, negotiation, alignment, centeredness and tranquility, joins paradoxically, like a zen *koan*, with the word "warrior", which expresses the energy of outer directedness, protection, boundary keeping and fighting. Together they combine to produce harmony, freedom and wholeness.

Queer folk inherently seem to hold a propensity towards the integration of these two polarities. In a sense, Queer folk often embody a two-spirit[2] worldview, and behave in a way that synthesizes these two energies.

A recent American hero was a gay man on Flight 93 on September 11, 2001. His actions along with other passengers of Flight 93 foiled the Al Qaeda attack that was intended to crash into Washington, DC. Mark Bingham acted as a Peaceful Warrior who offered his life to deter terrorist actions on that day when the world changed.

After the Iraqi war began, Queer folk, like the rest of the world, could be found taking bold stands as Peace Activists and military going to Iraq. A 21 year old gay marine reservist, Stephen Funk, became the first to refuse to participate in the US invasion of Iraq. He declared, "I will not obey an unjust war based on deception by our leaders".[3] Men at a Gay Men's Leadership Summit in up State New York spontaneously organized a gathering to bless those who went to Iraq and those who strongly opposed the war. The setting for this gathering was directly across the river from West Point. In a circle we shared stories of broken hearts, no matter which position we held. We seemed to represent the whole gamut of experience. One man spoke of his friend leaving for Iraq to serve, another man spoke of the pain from having served in the Gulf War.

Another spoke of those who went to be "body shields." Others held sacred those who were arrested by the thousands protesting and others just cried. We finished this circle by raising our hands out across the river to bless the men at West Point. Each of these snapshots captures a glimpse of the many responses Queer folk had to the initial understanding of going to war with Iraq. All of these modeled the warrior spirit with varying dimensions of peace. The more predominant picture of Queer folk was probably towards an antiwar position, yet honor was often held for all the disparate sides.

Whether the threat is perceived or actual fact, these outer expressions are indicators of the inner work of the peaceful warrior. Knowing ourselves is intimate. Creating dialogue across the divides within us and outside with others takes that kind of intimacy.

There are five defining themes of the Peaceful Warrior's role. The first is the ability to ask for help without shame or embarrassment. The second is the ability to be one's own authority, choosing the ground rules that define one's world and relationships. The third ability is the skill of dealing with conflict heartfully without abandoning personal power, and thereby acting with power and compassion whenever one sets or expands boundaries. The fourth ability is the skill of living fully in your "yes" or "no. The fifth skill is setting and expanding boundaries.

As one does the work of the Peaceful Warrior, the memories, habits and behavior patterns that have held us in bondage begin to drop away. For example, the shame, guilt and negative leftovers from childhood memories may keep their hold on us as belief patterns about our world. As we reframe our world to encompass the fullness of our human potential, they lose their power over us. The work of the Peaceful Warrior is to build self-knowledge and fear-lessly confront the emotions, situations, and relationships that cause him to "freeze-up," "shut down," or otherwise go numb. Because our bodies experience and retain vast amounts of infor-mation about our life, they are the repositories of great wisdom and guidance. A life fully lived will necessarily include ecstatic moments, both joyful and painful. Numbness is the nemesis of the Peaceful Warrior as he/she always strives to awaken the body to free it from numb existence.

Peaceful Warriors Are Survivors and Thrivers

The Peaceful Warrior is the image, the energy and the arche-type that will lead us as Queer men into greater healing, truth and freedom. Our history as Queer men has always been filled with men who were willing to face their fears with compassion and power. They have been men like you and me who:

1) ask for help.
2) are their own authority.
3) deal with conflict heartfully.
4) live in their "yes" or "no".
5) set or expand boundaries.

Our bodies respond to the ways of being a Peaceful Warrior by creating not only more well-being but often times healthier bodies. Evidence of this has been affirmed in many studies of men and women facing life-threatening diseases such as cancer and AIDS.[4] This research has shown that long-term survivors face their chal-lenges with both power and compassion—characteristics of the

Peaceful Warrior.

Of the approximately one hundred characteristics of long-term survivors here are a few:

Long-term survivors:

express feelings

listen to their bodies

are available to be in relationship and be sexually active

are true to themselves

are able to say "No", state their needs, ask for help

choose life, live passionately are present, in the moment

remember getting through other difficulties and traumas

are open to the use of alternative treatments

are politically active or altruistically involved

are spiritual (self-defined, not a part of a system that feels oppressive.)

experience a purpose of meaning in living

Moving From Victim to Survivor

In some ways those who identify as Queer folk have been Peaceful Warriors facing their internal and external obstacles. Few Queer people grew up in families, cultures, religious or political climates that celebrated them as Queer boys/men. Thus, the sense of safety to ask for help, being our own authority, saying "yes" or "no", dealing with conflict heartfully and setting boundaries has been fragile and felt easily threatened.

Facing our fears, even if it meant passing or avoiding, was a creative way of surviving. When anyone feels threatened the body responds by tightening up, breathing becomes either shallow or panicked and a general "pulling in" occurs. Both body and mind remember how to survive the threat and that memory becomes habit. Yet as adults, some of those ways no longer serve us well as they did in the past. In fact, they may create an atmosphere for disease and blocked intimacy.

As mentioned before, the psychology of the Peaceful Warrior resembles the characteristics of long term survivors. A simple model[5] I created encompassing the path of the Peaceful Warrior moves from the conditions a victim feels to the conditions of a survivor who thrives.

Safety in this model is a matter of perception. Victor Frankel, a World War II concentration camp survivor created a sense of safety during his internment by having a vision of himself teaching students the psychology of survival.[6] Safety, then, is internally felt and may not reflect the external reality of the moment. In a world that often threatens us as Queer people, safety as a felt body experience is one that few of us have ever experienced fully. The ways of the Peaceful Warrior may help us embrace a level of safety that transcends yet embodies physicality.

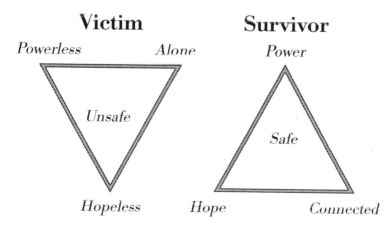

Victim

Powerless   *Alone*

Unsafe

Hopeless

Survivor

Power

Safe

Hope   *Connected*

27

Victim to Survivor

Charles Whitfield in his book, *Healing The Child Within*,[7] describes some characteristics of "safe" people. The experience of a "safe" versus an "unsafe" person is felt in our bodies. Using this information to bring healing or change is often the work of the Peaceful Warrior.

Some Characteristics of Safe & Unsafe People

Safe	Unsafe
Listen to you	Don't Listen
Hear You	Don't hear
Make eye Contact	No eye contact
Accept the real you	Reject
Validate the real you	Invalidate
Non-judgmental	Judgmental
Are real with you	False with you
Clear	Unclear
Boundaries negotiated	Boundaries unclear
Direct messages	Indirect Messages
No triangles*	Triangles in others
Supportive	Competitive
Loyal	Betray
Relationship authentic	Relationship feels contrived

*Triangles denote a model of third party indirect communication. Ownership is lost in the relationship and communication.

Ironically, the safe person can be as frightening to us as the person we categorize as an enemy. Listening to our bodies in the presence of safe and unsafe people may give indicate to us the steps needed to be taken to bring about change and greater inner free dom. In my work, I have witnessed many men who, after waking up to pleasure, begin to drop their grief only to suddenly feel frightened and then retreat emotionally. An open heart and an available body and spirit can feel vulnerable.

The way of the peaceful warrior is one of constant vulnerability through love and compassion. Yet, most of us forget that through our vulnerability we can find our power. Vulnerability often takes us to a physical shrinking and a smallness of energy. Finding ways to remember how big we are can help keep our heart open.

"Our deepest fear is not that we are inade-
quate. Our deepest fear is that we are pow-
erful beyond measure. It is our light, not
our darkness, that most frightens us. We
ask our selves who am I to be brilliant, gor-
geous, talented, fabulous? Actually who are
you not to be?

You are a child of God. Your playing small

does not serve the world. There is nothing

enlightening about shrinking, so that other

people won't feel unsure around you. We

were born to make manifest of glory of God

that is within us. It is not just in some of

us; it is in everyone.

As we let our own light shine, we uncon-

sciously give other people permission to do

the same. As we are liberated from our own

fear, our presence automatically liberates

others." 8

Marianne Williamson

Some years ago a group of 200 Queer people espousing a spiritual life) met with Rev. Jerry Falwell and 200 of his followers.9 The
Queer people took oaths before this meeting to adhere to tenants
of non-violence taught by Gandhi and Martin Luther King. Their
conversation focused on getting Falwell to stop his violent rhetoric
towards Queer people. Publicly, Jerry Falwell apologized for his

language of the past, even though he maintained his position which regarded Queer people as sinful. This monumental step with those who have been held as enemies causes us to look at the way of the Peaceful Warrior being one of power and compassion lending itself to potential change.

Coming Out

The phase "coming out" is a phrase used universally by Queer culture. Our "coming(s) out" as Queer people have been the actions of the Peaceful Warrior. Every "coming out" is one of moving from victim to survivor, thereby creating safety, hope, power and connectedness for ourselves no matter what the outcomes may be. These "coming(s) out", which are a constant process, lead to energetic change within ourselves and the world around us. This ecstatic path for the Peaceful Warrior requires coming out sexually, coming out spiritually, and finally coming out as an erotic spiritual being.

"Coming out" is a process of identity formation. It takes the spirit of the peaceful warrior to begin to unlayer one's true self from politics, religion, culture and family dynamics. Facing one's fears of approval or acceptance and taking a stand to be one's own authority requires bravery.

There are many coming out experiences we each face, no matter what our sexual orientation. Greg Louganis, former gold metal Olympic diver, tells his story of being in the spotlight of fame while examining his own life with the spotlight of the peaceful warrior. Greg has been public in coming out with his struggle from depression, being gay and living with AIDS.[10] Secrets are diffused by being known. Greg modeled power and compassion to face his fears of destigmatizing depression and AIDS and celebrating his

31

sexual orientation.

I submit that the Queer movement and Queer people have just begun to discover their true identity as individuals and as a tribe. Subtly and not so subtly, there is a form of Stockhom Syndrome[11] that Queer folk must work through. Loyalty to one's abuser becomes normalized because the abuser has shown care or nurture. This unraveling is often a complicated web to disentangle.

As a young man, I had many powerful mystical experiences within what was known as the Charismatic Renewal in the Christian Church. It was a movement in the 1970's that crossed all denominations in the United States. My experiences in this movement were ecstatic (just as were my first sexual encounters with men). In fact, the feelings in my body of rushes of energy were clearly the same for me.

My body knew the truth that the erotic and spiritual were the same, yet the Christian culture around me did not support that truth. My Charismatic teachers were powerful men and women who often had psychic abilities and whose energetic touch literally healed people. They spoke boldly as they proclaimed their understanding of biblical texts and they also loved me deeply. These dynamics of care, power and truth (which I felt within my body) created my personal Stockholm Syndrome.

In this movement, I became a young leader and I was seen as a pastor within this new configuration of church. My passion for God was a soaring experience and my passion to connect to gay men was also soaring within me. I had not been able to see that these passions were the same energies, so, of course, I created (unconsciously) a spiritual crisis for myself to face the truth. I decided to take a sabbatical "being led" to join a charismatic community in Ft. Lauderdale, Florida. In Ft. Lauderdale were some powerful

Charismatic teachers and a community whose worship stirred my soul. Also, in Ft. Lauderdale was a large gay community, the pleasures of which I had tasted before on Spring Break. It was not difficult to see I was forcing myself to confront what I really knew to be the truth and integrate my worlds. Savvy to my struggle, one of my teachers, a man who was strongly psychic, was distraught with my decision to leave for Ft. Lauderdale. This man who demonstrated many gifts of healing wanted to "pray over" me before I left for Ft. Lauderdale. He laid his hands on my head and prophesied, "Kirk, as you drive your car across the bridge (to leave for Ft. Lauderdale from Ohio) you will die." This may sound ridiculous to some, but for me this was an extremely powerful, spiritual man.

Following my own guidance to listen to my own drumbeat, I remember clearly gripping the steering wheel of my car, taking a deep breath and driving across the Singing Bridge between Ohio and Kentucky headed for Florida. Of course, I didn't die, but then, on the other hand, maybe I did. In that action, I proclaimed to the universe that I was my own authority and I was following my truth, not someone else's truth. Some energetic links to a chain of bondage had been broken and old body stories of a " high tolerance for inappropriate behavior,"* the need for approval and the need to take care of others before myself had been healed.

Yet my own personal "jihad" inside was not over. I had already learned a basic principle in behavioral medicine, human consciousness studies and my experience with healers and shamans. The notion is that symptoms of cancer, heart disease or an emotional scar may appear completely healed, but if the inner work that caused the symptom is not cleared, the symptom will return

*Characteristic of psychic wounding from Charles Whitfield's book, *Healing the Child Within*

again. My experience of driving across the bridge empowered me greatly in my ability to discern my own truth. Although I had empowered myself, I had not realized that being gay is a gift.

The magic of my erotic explorations continued to inform my soul of the sacredness of being gay. I recall having a sexual experience with a man who had tennis elbow. His arm hurt constantly. As we played erotically, feelings like I had many times praying flowed through my body. After this pleasurable sexual encounter, the man told me the chronic pain he had in his elbow was gone. Even all this was not enough to step out of the Christian dogma I was told that homosexuality was a broken state of being. Trying so hard to be liberated from my gay life, I went off to a deprogramming training in the suburbs of Washington, D.C. there I finally "got it." No matter how much prayer, fasting, scriptures study, support groups and self-denial, I saw or heard from the teacher and students of this program to "fix" gay men, they all still remained gay in orientation. My next step as a peaceful warrior was to again speak my truth, that being gay was a sacred design and expression of spirit. The final layers of those body stories were being cleared away. At this time, I had become an intern on staff at a conservative Charismatic Evangelical Presbyterian Church of two thousand members. This time, telling my truth meant sharing it with people who had loved me for ten years but whose beliefs, however, invalidated what Don Clark would call "my gay truth." Embracing my gay truth created a personal schism with them that matched the divergence in our beliefs. This loss was the last step in my freedom and recovery from this personal Stockholm Syndrome. My body now knew ecstasy with all of its sorrow and joy. I now embraced my whole identity, yet experienced the grief it caused, that of leaving old friends and old ways of living.

This action of identity formation, moving from victim to survivor (becoming a peaceful warrior) cleared the path (for my integration of the spiritual and the sexual, and led me to recognize, practice, and celebrate my gifts as a sexual healer. Loving myself initially meant unlayering the internalized oppressions I had accepted as truth. At some point in most people's lives, certainly in mine, the personal journey is less about clearing the old stories of a pseudo-identity and more about writing a new identity that sings the deepest song of the heart.

One of those moments took place for me in 1986 at a Gay Spirit Visions conference in Highlands, North Carolina. It was at this conference I met James Broughton, Andrew Ramer, Rocco Pratt, Joseph Kramer, John Stowe and Sequoia Thom Lundy. These men's teachings, ideas and encouragement allowed me to name myself out loud as a sexual healer.

Identities often are solidified in a ritual moment (conscious or not) and so it was that weekend. Gay ecstatic and poet James Broughton spent the weekend developing his ideas that the body is sacred and that the way we use it as gay men is sacred work. He facilitated a ritual for about twenty men who disrobed and formed two concentric circles, one facing out, one facing in. As we stood, paired and looking into each others eyes, we found the sacred in each other. With each pairing, we connected through gentle exercises, both physical and mental. As we moved in turn to the next man in the circle, Broughon directed us in respectful touch, hands over each other's hearts, and in communicating with words our perception of the other man's sacredness: "your erotic energy is sacred," "holy," "healing," "powerful." Finally, James had us hold each others penises and testicles while still retaining a connection from the heart. Somehow, in these moments, I knew my life had integrated a call from Spirit that I had heard my whole life. A whole spirituality was born anew in me, an erotic spirituality that held my body, my sexuality and my erotic expression as the extension of the divine. After the weekend conference was over, a few of the men and I went to a neighboring white water river and baptized ourselves as sexual healers. What a grand coming out this truth has made for the ministry of my life.

Coming out may at times be a coming out into solidarity, such as solidarity with anyone who is still disenfranchized. Throughout my life, inclusiveness, human rights and civil rights have guided my path. During the beginning of the war in Iraq, I registered myself and Flesh and Spirit Community in support of Arab-Americans and Muslims who were being looked at differently by mainstream American culture. I remember how right that simple action felt in my body while cognitively giving me pause for at own fears that a political Big Brotherism was developing in the U.S.

Solidarity demands inclusion. Truly knowing ourselves puts us in a comfortable space to stand, allowing solidarity to be a simple action of "yes." I'll close this section on coming out as a peaceful warrior with this inclusive experience that sweetly speaks to identity formation being healing.

Shadow was the first transgendered man to come to Flesh and Spirit Community. The story started for me at an intake interview for our *Peaceful Warrior* workshop. After 45 minutes of asking Shadow questions about his body stories related to facing his fears, it was time to do the experiential part of the intake interview: "So in this part, we are going to do some touch with your shirt off," I said. His response to that was "before I take my shirt off, I need to tell you something." I had no idea Shadow was a transgendered man. My journey of inclusion was about to go to a new level. I had worked just 2 weeks prior with my first transgendered man in my bodywork practice. Now, the moment of welcoming transgendered brothers into our community seemingly was knocking on my door. My heart was pounding and chills raised the hair on my arms. I knew this was truly a gift from Spirit for me and for all the transgendered brothers who were to follow in this man's footsteps.

Following the interview and the Peaceful Warrior workshop, Shadow assisted me in a training for all the men of Flesh and Spirit. The training was focused on the stories of our bodies and using pleasure as a pathway to healing. Shadow showed each man how to touch his body informing them of what was pleasurable for him. I cried. I was so moved at Shadow's story of congruence and the openness of each man truly naked in their truth with each other. We all "came out" and were healed that night

On the inner plane, the Peaceful Warrior is listening deeply to his/her body to remember the ways of healing for one's self and the world. On the outer plane, the Peaceful Warrior's actions may be seen bringing light to places of injustice, where the body of the earth and her people are being wounded or oppressed.

News journalists like Anderson Cooper, Christiane Amanpour, or the late Richard Pearl, can often be seen shining a light on places where severe conflict, disaster and lack of attention are being highlighted. Anderson Cooper's news program called "Anderson Cooper's 360" has a buzz phrase of "Keeping them honest." Anderson's willingness to publicly disclose difficult issues like the suicide of his brother and his willingness to challenge authorities around issues of injustice offer a glimpse of the way of the peaceful warrior. Anderson says, "Loss is a theme that I think a lot about, and it's something in my work that I dwell on. I think when you experience any kind of loss, especially the kind I did, you have questions about survival: Why do some people thrive in situations that others can't tolerate? Would I be able to survive and get on in the world on my own?"[12] The questions Anderson asks are the essence of the Peaceful Warrior's quest of surviving and thriving. Calling forth action by simply spotlighting the facts moves people to respond.

The action of the Peaceful Warrior is to be honest with oneself first and to insist on honesty in the world. The ways we insist are the cutting edge for the Peaceful Warrior. Insisting that justice be done while offering understanding and compassion are delicate petals to flowers of peace.

The Lover

The path of the Peaceful Warrior begins a process of self-love that naturally leads to the second archetype, the Lover, an archetype of intimacy and intimacies. The Lover calls Queer folk to honor all of their partners, past, present and future. Honoring love relationships of any kind allows us to drop our grief and melt the hardness of the heart. This preparation of the heart leads us to offer our gifts of healing to others. In the Queer world, the archetype of the Lover offers the possibility of creating contractual relationships of intimacy that may be more congruently than traditional models. This new model of the lover allows the script to be written with equality, where each person gets to take full responsibility for themselves, thus being fully available for intimacy.

The ongoing cultural conversation about gay marriage is certainly relevant to the idea of writing our own intimacy scripts. There have always been more models to relationships than those being advocated by religious fundamentalism. Queer relationships may have been easier to dismiss when they were seen only about sex, but the gay marriage conversation has invited us to look at contracts of intimacy and how we wish to express them.

My own marriage to my husband was not a political act, but a statement of our love for each other and a desire to complement each other's journey of Spirit for as long as we are in these bodies. The conversation of intimacy seems vital to the Queer movement, not only as a political question, but as a question of our relationship to the earth.

The kind of relationship and intimacy contracts one may choose are relevant only to the integrity of the contracts, not to an external system of morals. Open, closed, polyamorous, monogamous, or behaviorally exclusive relationships are energetic contracts based on congruence. Telling our truth about intimacies of all kinds may be how we as Queer folk expecially help heal the world.

Since our marriage ritual, our hearts, bodies and spiritual missions seem to have merged for me. Perhaps this is because when we bless something, it is changed. A blessing is a statement of intent and congruence that then guides our evolution. So may we bless all the configurations of truth that emerge as lovers.

In the Flesh and Spirit workshops called *The Lover*, we list as many people as we can with whom we have been intimate in any way, especially in sexual relationships with other men. As we do this, patterns and challenges surrounding intimacy begin to appear, but so does a willingness to forgive ourselves or any partners in the process. We spend the day listening to our bodies to help us know how we feel about blessing all our past relationships and how available we feel to welcome intimacy into our lives now. Blessing relationships of the past changes the energy they hold for us in the present.

John Ballew has worked with Flesh and Spirit Community around the archetype of The Lover. He prefaced his experiential body exercise with us by acknowledging the study of Franklin Abbott[13] around fathers of gay men and their relationships to their sons. Abbott found that fathers of gay men often felt separated from their sons by age 3. John Ballew then used that information to guide a healing exercise, by having one man role-play the father, by holding or cradling the other man, who played the role of son. The son was able to tell the father what he wanted to hear from his father, and how he wanted to be held. The father obliged, allowing the son to practice revising the body stories around the relationship with his actual father. Such a simple exercise surfaced rich material and stories for the men doing this exercise. Intimacy with the father seems like an important piece of work for Queer men in their partnerships with other men.

A profound expansion of this exercise was carried out by a Queer friend of mine I had worked with early in the AIDS epidemic. Andy was his name, a young man with AIDS in his twenties doing clear consciousness healing work. Andy, who felt estranged from his father, wanted to finish whatever business he could with his father and asked his father to clear the slate with him. After sharing many formerly unsaid words with each other, Andy asked his father to get naked with him and hold him. As you might imagine, they did this together crying the whole time.

The Sufi mystic Rumi says, "The agony of lovers is the doorway to God."[14] Clearing through grief like Andy did allows one to be available to intimacy and healing that is truly ecstatic.

Queer folk have great potential to help heal the world as we do our own grief work. Much of the world's conflicts seem to be about peoples, nations, religious and governments stuck in their grief of what was supposed to be. Being seen and known without barriers, i.e., intimacy, may be the answer to world conflict.

In 2002, the city of Jerusalem conducted LGBT Pride Day parades and celebrations.[15] Images of Arab/Muslim men and women with their Israeli/Jewish partners showed that Queer intimacy goes beyond the boundaries of generational wounds, nationalism and religious prohibitions. The archetype of the Lover builds upon the actions of the Peaceful Warrior demonstrating the possibilities of harmony.

"From the beginning of my life I have been looking for your face"[16]   *Rumi*

The Sacred Prostitute

The gift of service is governed by the archetype of the Sacred Prostitute. The Sacred Prostitute is a unique and powerful type of healer. The Sacred Prostitute calls forth the full potential of the heart, soul and body to awaken. He/she uses erotic touch, compassionate listening, and a total commitment to living within the body to guide others to freedom and healing. It is said of the Sacred Prostitutes of the past that "...everything she/he touches changes." The Sacred Prostitute guides us into ways of physical and emotional touch that transform and bless, touch that knows no separation between Flesh and Spirit. The service of the Sacred Prostitute was a wedding with the Divine through the body.

Although the Sacred prostitute archetype is not exclusive to gender, it clearly has attributes of the Divine Feminine. In her book, *The Sacred Prostitute*, Nancy Qualls-Corbett described an

imaginary scene from antiquity like this: "Imagine the sacred prostitute greeting the stranger, a world weary man who has come to
the temple to worship the goddess of love. No words are spoken;
her outstretched arms and the soft warm expression of her radiant
eyes say what needs to be said. In her private chambers, the sacred
love room of the temple, filled with the fragrance of herbs and
flowers, she bathes the stranger, offering him balm...In the near
darkness, alone in her rapture, she performs the ritual of lighting
the perfumed oil lamp, gently swaying and chanting softly in
prayer of thanksgiving to the goddess...The woman and the
stranger know the consummation of the love act is consecrated by
the deity through which they are renewed."[17]

The energy of the Divine Feminine seems integral to healing
the planet today. This archetype of the feminine embodied by
Queer people (of all genders) may reconnect the sacred with the
erotic, in a counter-motion to that of fundamentalists who wish to
separate sex and Spirit.

I use the term Sacred Prostitute purposefully. There are many
names used over the millennia to describe those servants of the
Divine: sexual shaman, sexual healer, tantrika, sacred whore, temple prostitute, holy one and sacred intimate. "Sacred prostitute" is
the ancient term which seems to hold the charge of unifying the
polarities of flesh and spirit. (All of them may be interchange-
able.).

The following Gnostic text ("The Thunder, Perfect Mind,"
from the Nag Hamaddi Library) demonstrates one of the greatest
powers of the Divine Feminine, the power to contain seeming
polarities in a unified whole:

For I am the first and the last.

I am the honored and the scorned one.

I am the whore and the holy one.

I am the wife and the virgin.

I am the mother and the daughter.

I am the members of my mother.

I am the silence that is incomprehensible

and the idea whose remembrance is frequent.

I am the voice whose sound is manifold

and the word whose appearance is multiple.

I am the utterance of my name. [18]

The energies of midwiving at birth, at death, during disease, creating contraception/birth control and perpetuating the old religion of Goddess and God in harmony are all ways the different waves of the Sacred Prostitute archetype have manifested through the ages.

Along with the care of large numbers of folks and thousands of Lesbians, Queer men demonstrated the actions of the Sacred Prostitute during the severest AIDS years. Teaching safer sex, providing condoms/dental dams, massage, energy work, erotic work and being midwives to the dying were ancient images breaking forth in recent times.

The world's population in 2001 was estimated at 6.1 billion people, and projected to be over 9 billion by 2050. [19] Innately most Queer people have not contributed greatly to that population explosion. So, like the Sacred Prostitutes of the past, GLBT people seem to minimize the population by having fewer children. I would propose that we see this as Nature's (or the Goddess's) gift to the planet: a natural form of contraception, of which the sacred prostitutes were the guardians in antiquity.

Additionally, when Queer folk have chosen to have children (through a variety of means) or by adoption, there is a very deliberate intention to care for a child. Some early behavioral science literature around Lesbian and Gay parents suggests that the children often feel very wanted by their parents because they were so deliberately chosen. Certainly the literature is clear that children growing up with queer partners are no more or less healthy than heterosexual families.

On many levels, the sacredness of bodies is being expressed uniquely through Queer people today in actions associated with the archetype of the Sacred Prostitute.

The Elder

The Elder weaves together the wisdom and energies of the Peaceful Warrior, Lover and Sacred Prostitute. The Elder is the archetype of mature love. His/her work fosters inclusion, justice and integration. The Elder is a particularly powerful archetype to invoke in "modern" societies, where Elders are often bereft of family and community. Many tribal cultures around the world recognize a close affinity between the very young and the very old. Just as the newly born emerge from a different consciousness and are therefore very close to different states of reality, so is the Elder close to these different states as they prepare to merge once again with Spirit.

Queer people have a legitimate craving for true Elders in their lives. The process of coming out often is embarked upon as a solo effort. The absence of loving guidance and mentoring in our lives can cause much unnecessary struggle. True Elders recognize this and provide mentoring as a healing remedy. Moreover, it is important to note that Elderhood can be achieved at young ages, especially when an entire community faces adversity together. For this reason, many Queer people are called to be Elders outside their own communities, giving care and guidance to many different kinds of people.

The Elder usually has lived his/her life fully enough to know the difference between what is true for the individual and a Spiritual truth that sees beyond the self. In young aspirants of truth, this knowledge of eldership may appear to be more a re-membering beyond their years of wisdom stored in the energy (it may be the DNA) of their bodies. This wisdom of discernment sets The Elder apart to be a leader and overseer in the community.

In the current news world, words like "liar", "misled", "misinformation", "deceit" and "premeditated" are common language. How refreshing to consider "yes" meaning "yes," "no" meaning "no" and "I don't know" to be an honest assessment. Since Queer folk have been a part of the every tribe throughout history, we are privy to possible wisdom that bridges the worlds that divide us.

Malidoma Some speaks of gatekeepers[20] within the African Dagara tribe who are the bridge builders between the living and the ancestors. They are gay/queer men, (although they would not call themselves that) who bring the wisdom of the ancestors to the tribe. Malidoma reports that gatekeepers go into their caves and do ecstatic ritual to open to the voices of the spirits.

In the community of Flesh and Spirit many seem to be stepping into this place of leadership. A model to our community can easily be seen in the guidance of Dr. Don Clark, who has shared wisdom with us over the years. Don's principle teaching to gay men has been to share one's "gay truth". Well-known for his book, *Loving Someone Gay*,[21] Don's new memoir, *Becoming Someone Gay*, offers the story of a living elder to Queer men.

One of the gay truths Don Clark challenges gay men to face is their shame. Facing the truth of your shame, e.g., that it is often a vestige of someone else's shame acting upon you, creates freedom

from shame when it is not appropriate, while also acknowledging the usefulness of shame when it seems warranted. This has been "Elder wisdom" to a hungry community. Imagine acknowledging shame in yourself and being fully free of it. Then imagine teaching the world to acknowledge shame and being free of it. What would that world look like? The role of the Elder teaches what he/she knows for wholeness in the community.

"Tell your gay truth"
Don Clark

The elder is inseparable from community. The Elder also must know he/she belongs in community. This healing that often needs to take place before one becomes an elder. As I once heard a famous spiritual teacher talk about gay men, he spoke of a sense of cruelty and judgment that at times can be found within the gay culture. My assessment is that this cruelty is ultimately a fear of not being a part of community.

Another beauty of the work of erotic body prayer and communities like Flesh and Sprit is how the body is honored in all of its stages of aging. Yet, the truth of such acceptance may be an ongoing process of re-writing the culturally inculcated stories of our bodies.

I heard Malidoma Somé speak once saying the wrinkles on the face of an Elder were honored, recognized and expected. Finding beauty in all things may be the highest value and truth the Elder can remind us of.[22]

The Mystic

The fifth archetype in the cycle is the Mystic. The Mystic integrates the skills, practices and wisdom of the other four archetypes. The Mystic is in union with the Divine. His/her path is one of exploring, seeking, and meeting with Spirit in all things. The integrated truth of "I am" is the domain where the Mystic seeks to live. The Mystic invites the experience of wonder, unity and ecstasy into the mundane world, healing our minds from the flurry and clutter of our lives. The Mystic knows in the Divine. He/she flows all possibilities.

"the body is sacred"
Walt Whitman

Mystics often appear foolish. When one finds that Goddess/God, the divine and the holy are in all things, it is very difficult to have enemies. Rumi constantly spoke of his passion for the Beloved. The Beloved was the face of everyone and everything.

In altered states of ecstatic work, it is often easy to feel one with all things. The challenge of the Mystic is to see the divine in those with whom you disagree, whom you oppose, or whom you find viscerally disgusting. Being a Mystic does not invalidate the boundaries and clear commitment to equality and justice expressed by the Peaceful Warrior. It is a choice to hold all as things sacred.

Before she died, I heard Mother Teresa of Calcutta speak. She was asked how she dealt with "burn out" seeing suffering everyday. Her response was "that is not my experience. I find it a privilege to do this work for each face is the face of Christ."[23]

In a workshop, I asked participants to notice what they felt in their bodies as they sent loving intention or prayer to those they loved. Although some sense of empathic pain or concern for the person often registered in participant's bodies, the overall feelings were, of course, joyful. Then, I had them spend time sending love and peace to George W. Bush and then to Osama Bin Laden, and to notice what they registered in their bodies with each of these. It was clear for all that the Mystic's state of being one with all was easy in concept, but the specifics of reality revealed work yet to be done.

The Prophet

The first and last major archetype in this progression frames both the beginning and the end of the ecstatic path in this archetypal journey. The messenger or herald is the model for this archetype. It brings us back to the beginning of the cycle. The Prophet/Prophetess is our messenger or herald.

It is humorous that the rabbinical meanings of the Hebrew word for prophet sound very Queer. The word "nabi"[24] means "to speak enthusiastically, to utter cries and to more or less make wild gestures" like pagans. The Torah uses the word as "interpreter or mouthpiece" often describing the function of the word as "prophetic knowledge and vision."

One could entertain many spiritual or philosophical ideas about Queer identity and origins. One I assert is that being Queer is a gift and a sacred part of the whole. Biologist Thomas Huxley said, "No negative trait (one that does not reproduce) ever continues to appear in a given species millennium after millennium after millennium unless it in some way serves the survival of the species."[25]

In line with that assertion, I might also open the possibility that our consciousness chose to come to the earth as Queer. No matter whether this is true or not, the very nature of the Queer person is prophetic.

In my sessions with Shimakataya (my non-physical spirit guide that manifested after my London experience), the following was said of Queer people, Queer spirituality and the archetype of the Prophet. These words may resonate with you as a literal prophecy, as metaphors, or even a dream. Whether you hold them as fact or fiction does not seem as important as what they awaken in you.

My partner, Donny, begins this conversation by asking questions of Shimakataya. (This is an accumulation of three different sessions with Shimakataya).

D: Might you speak to the theme of Queer Spirituality?

S: Yes, this is clearly a topic, a theme, an energy about which we wish to speak, to open up the eyes of the blind, the ears of the deaf; to bring about a new sight and a new hearing.

Indeed, this is a place of confusion for many whereas it is intended to be a place of enlightenment for all. So we are happy to speak with you today and many times around this particular theme. You will be able to write volumes around this theme highlighting ideas coming from each segment of our conversation with you. So we might begin today by giving you just a small amount.

The nature of Queer spirituality, as you might expect, has many different stories to it. It is not just one story. Thus, those who would reduce it to one story simply are missing the tapestry and beauty coming together in this age. It has not always been the same as it is today. The gathering of Queer people, as you call them, is unique in this time though it has threads and currents of past time stories in it. We would bring forth an idea that seems foreign to you. You are well aware of the world events: from the disaster of 9/11 to Katrina to the disasters of the mud slides in the Philippines. Those disasters represent souls who are, on some level, choosing to be released from the planet not as individuals, but as groups. We would have you pay attention. You will continue to hear of large groups of people leaving the planet together who may not have apparent commonality around what they in their conscious minds call values or history. This is much of what is happening today with Queer spirituality. Those who have died in the past are coming together and reincarnating in groups to serve some common purpose.

For example, as Kirk has intuited, the witches killed in the past as individuals or groups were really enlightened healers who were trying to anchor the light between heaven and earth; much as many Queer people are beginning to understand as their role: to anchor the light in the Earth's new transformation. Consequently, groups of people from past generations are coming back as a collective called Queer. Some of them had different functions in the past, but all of them coming now have a common mission to be light-bearers on the planet. This is possible because they have had past lives as all genders. In addition, they bring a spectrum of understanding and experience that is unique to Queer people. As Kirk often says, they can bridge the worlds.

Queer people have shown up in every family, race, culture, religion and place on the earth. Thus, they bring with them the full knowledge and experience of what each culture has offered both in its shadow realm as well as in its healing realm. We are beginning to paint for you what is a very complex picture that can be reduced down to a common calling Queer people have today. They are bringing together the polarities that are filled with strife at this time. Queer people have experienced all these polarities at some place at some time. Thus, the understanding is deeply embedded in the body's DNA, as you speak of it. That provides the bridge for people to find commonality. It is the bridge of commonality essential in this age that often feels so divisive and split.

So we have started our conversation with you about the complex energies and ideas that we wish to address further with you. We will give you yet just another tidbit: the topic of gender, sex, and body. The underlying topic is healing. Those three things are unique to queer people in that information has accumulated over lifetimes through their reincarnated bodies. Now, those Queer people are coming back to bring about an awareness of the sacred body of the earth—the sacred body from which all channels of light ascend.

There is a part of this present collective called Queer that is not from this planet and was not incarnated and reincarnated repeatedly on the Earth, but who are choosing to come be bridge builders with this collective. They have a slightly different vibration of service that is not about working out what you call Karma or soul issues. So they are not bringing that into the collective. So in that sense they stand with and even act as leaders in the collective because they are not trying to work out past life concerns that have not been finished and resolved. These Queer people came

51

clearly to be servants of the planet at this time. And they knew coming as a Queer person they might bring about a different voice that could help bring the bridges the chasm of what you call the right and the left. Does this mean polarities?

The last theme we would leave you with is another function of Queer people. Queer folk are clearly a tribal people who have come from a variety of collectives for a common purpose at this time. One of these purposes activated through Queer spirituality is that the norms, standards, conventions of time, place and location are disrupted by the very energy of those who are Queer. This breaks open some of the underlying issues needing to be cleared.

So their very presence, whether they call themselves activists, gay, lesbian, transgender, questioning or other names begins to disrupt what you call the norms and standards of the institutions and the ideologies energetic in all places. That disruption, in turn allows for issues to come forth that need attention for the planet to come into its evolution of healing and of light.

D: I feel that's the role I played in my own family.

S: Yes, it is so. You were disturbing to them.

D: Yes, I was.

S: And they, on some level, knew that the disturbance was for their benefit. And even though there were times of what appeared to be resistance, in the deepest parts of themselves there was an acknowledgement that something special had been brought to them, through them; and they welcomed that. So it was a deliberate unconscious choice on their part to bring you into the family to disrupt, so more healing could take place on this realm for the work to be activated on an escalated level as they passed into the next realm. So I am aware of presences of Mommy and Daddy as you call them. And they thank you for being born as a Queer person to bring about the disruption so that they might be healed more fully and completely and in a more rapid way. You have been a gift.

The story that was just spoken and affirmed is just a highlight of queer stories around how disturbance comes naturally. Even though it may be met with extreme resistance, the disturbance in and of itself produces a level of healing. Obviously, if the resistance can be dropped, the bridge can be opened and healing can take its full potential. But even if the resistance is not dropped fully, the disturbance alone provides healing.

And so we say thank you for opening this conversation and introducing this theme into this body of work that will be helpful not only to Queer people but also to those wishing to understand the role of Queer people and their spiritual mission on this planet in this particular time.

We have given you some things to chew on.

D: Can you speak to the Prophet archetype?

S: Yes, the work Kirk is doing at this time around the archetypes has a fuller meaning than he is aware of. And so he is following his intuition to speak of these archetypes. Archetypes themselves hold a richness of unconscious material which brings both the light and shadow. There is no way for the consciousness to fully wrap around each one of these archetypes for their very emergence is, in part, hidden.

Thus having said that, we would speak to the archetype of the Prophet, as he is a messenger who is a herald. Kirk is trying to sort out the role of Queer peoples, especially of Queer men, how this archetype of the prophet is relevant. And what we would come back to is some of what we were speaking to you about Queer spirituality and the questions you addressed us formerly about. The role of the Prophet is helping to prepare the way with others to welcome and anchor the light of evolution of the earth. As Queer folk, there are many who are ready and able to speak their truth in love of their visions, but they are frightened to do so. This fear must be eliminated and integrated into their beings so that they can boldly pronounce that which they can see and hear. They know in the core of their being, there was a message implanted in them as they chose to arrive on the earth as Queer. Thus, that prophetic nature was what we were speaking to you about when we said all Queer people, no matter what their origins, have a common mission: bringing about disturbance. However this is not a disturbance just for disturbance sake, but a shaking of the foundation, helping the eruption of truth to come forth in this process. Those still holding on in the right or the left, in the black or the white or, in other extremes of the polarities, might find a peaceful way of experiencing the whole and honoring the whole.

Queer people have a prophetic role to serve which relates to our mission with you. We have chosen to work with Kirk specifically to help open eyes, open ears and to bring voice to people who do not see or hear or have voice. Thus part of the role of Queer people on the Earth is to see who the marginalized people are—those who are under the hands of oppression—to help bring about for them a net of safety so that they might feel a sense of sanctuary so that they might be able to step out of the slavery they might feel from others.

The role of the Prophet is often dubious in that a Prophet may speak one thing and then another might happen. This is because the role of the prophet is simply to bring possibilities into awareness so people can energetically come to a course correction and come more fully into the flow of the Divine Nature. Thus a Prophet or Prophetess has the role to bring forth a message that opens up the potential of healing.

As we have said before, there are those coming to the Earth to serve. Only a few have been born at this time, but there will soon be more coming who do not have an agenda of correcting their karmic patterns or working out past lifetime agendas, but simply coming to provide light, healing and conditions of healing for those who are most marginalized.

These new leaders are not bound by a politic. They are bound to the love of the Divine which sent them. And because they are unencumbered they will be truly leaders and avatars of the planet and they will be fully recognized, as it has been in other times, to be a part of the Queer tribe that is honored and revered. And their words and actions, although they do not wish visibility, will be often noticed quite significantly.

We spoke last time about the energy of disturbance in context to the words of sex, gender and body as healing. There are more sexes than male and female. There is more of a spectrum to be expressed in physical form and in energetic form. It is confounding and disturbing to those that wish to hold onto their polarized ideas. For them, to step out of their rigid ideas would undermine their very ways of thinking and thus they would have to start over again, causing great fear.

So the idea of sex and gender and body as healing are primary places where Queer folk in this age have the automatic appearance as the disturbance-makers. They provoke questions about sex, orientation and expression. They provoke questions about genders: how many genders and how gender is to be expressed. They also bring attention to the body, all of its stories, its shadows, and are about reclaiming one's original essence. The body is an expression of the divine, the work has to do with shedding the stories of self-hatred held in the body as a result of abuses that are so predominate across all peoples.

So as we have spoken about these expressions as disturbance they are the attention-getters. But these attention-getters are only on the surface of what the true mission is for Queer people. The attention may be to shake the foundation. Once the foundation is shaken, then the prophetic truths of Queer nature emerge. This will enable visions of peace, harmony and cooperation among all races, peoples and all beings and all of creation to be affirmed and actualized.

There will be others besides us speaking to some of what we have said about these new seeds of enlightenment that are coming through the Queer community. The purpose is not only to heal the planet and larger community but also to raise up the greatest and highest potential out of the tribe of Queer people to come into the fore and be the brightest light.

We hesitate to give a name to these new folks, for names often begin to formulate and create a function, a whole construct by which one operates. Thus the part becomes a self-fulfilling prophecy as it has been spoken (e.g. the children coming as the Indigo children, Crystal children). We hesitate to give a name to these Queer folks at this time because the expanse of their mission is not to be so diminutive.

D: Perhaps we can continue the conversation about Queer spirituality?

S: We are happy to go further with the information about Queer Spirituality so that you can compile more information so that your readers and listeners might better understand what we are saying. That will help to free them more fully.

As we have spoken of the New Ones who are coming as avatars and leaders as Queer people not attached to the Queer movement but on a mission of bringing light to the whole of the Earth in common with all the universal forces of well-being. Those of you who are on a journey as Queer people will feel a new electricity in your bodies. Your energy and your participation as this level of disturbance we spoke of (that is a part of your very nature) will also bring you up as more interactions happen from above and from below. These New Ones are coming to hold space with you. As you do your work in clearing out old images of guilt, shame, sorrow, grief and compassion (that is, not truly a real compassion but a

holding of the sorrow, guilt and shame together that sometimes gets fused). As these things are released more and more there will be a space for the Queer movement to come into its true spiritual nature and as in many native cultures, the Queer people will again be seen as the folks who bring about change in peaceful, harmonious, joyful, and playful ways.

The Earth needs this movement of Queer spirituality to awaken those who call themselves Queer into their full identity. Much of the identity of Queer people has been cloaked for so long in the constrictions of the culture which has caused a "forgetting" of who you really are. In their remembering of who they really are Queer people will break out of the culture again to be the disturbance of love, and thus awakening the planet into more healing. This will be exemplified by Queer people doing what you call social justice actions in much more clear ways than ever have been demonstrated on the Earth before. Ways that you call altruistic and even philanthropic will be promulgated in the Queer culture as you see an awakening that reaches out beyond the limits of Queer culture itself. This will come with a new consciousness which will be indeed about telling the truth at levels which the planet is not used to at this time. And that truth-telling will come from a place of compassion and love. There will be again greater and greater disturbances. It's like the tsunami that brought about destruction, but the destruction is only allowing a new buildup. And those who have left from the tsunami are indeed some of those who chose to be recycled. Some of them are coming back as Queer people because they were more advanced in their knowing already.

The ancient wisdom of the ancestors is something that is in the bodies of all people and in Queer people. Since that ancient wisdom is so available, the more queer people acknowledge the sacredness of the body, the more they will emancipate not only themselves, but also those who are in shackles of slavery around being in body. Many religious cultures hold that the body is just a nuisance and we would affirm the body is the expression of the divine. It has chosen itself and thus cherish it, honor it and give pleasure to it.

These are some glimpses to assimilate and put together in your composition of Queer spirituality that may be different in language to what some others have spoken.

D: Regarding the ancestors: I find the cemeteries are a good

place for my music. In our recent trip to Hawaii, for example I enjoyed playing in the Koloa cemetery. Any comment on the work in the cemeteries, or a way to proceed?

S: We would bridge both topics regarding what you have spoken of and the notion of Queer spirituality and how it is embedded in some of what Kirk and you are doing: being attentive to the ancestors, especially to the souls who have not yet furthered their transition to the Greatest Good in order to benefit themselves and the tapestry we call the Universal Life Force or Consciousness. This is also an aspect of the Queer vibration. What you have done in being in the cemetery playing and holding space is to welcome the ancestors. You allowed them a gentle way of gathering together and to be reminded that there is more than what has been shrouded in the veil around them. The music actually created a vibration, a gentle vibration that set the stage for their awareness so that they might go further on the journey. We would advocate you do this whenever you feel inspired to. And you will know when those moments are to go not only to cemeteries but there are many pockets of energetic holding spaces in the planet in open and contained areas where souls are wandering somewhat aimlessly.

We will offer that part of this work is the bridge-building that Queer people in general have to offer the planet at this time. Healing both the land and clearing those energies that are trapped so that they might be free to benefit themselves and help bring healing to the polarities. This is part of the design of Queer people. So play when you feel like playing. Play when it seems somewhat odd to others to play, for it is not them you are playing for, it is for the trapped energies. And we would give you a broader image to hold: the trapped energies are not only the souls of the depart-

ed bodies, but energies you do not have any words for but are part of that mesh.

D: Thank you. The other thing we were aware of in Hawaii was that many of the waiters and waitresses we drawn to us and asked for Tarot readings. It seemed there was a population we were being invited to work with which we gladly did. So the question: is there something there for us in Hawaii or was that just something that happens as we walk through the world?

S: Yes, there are several ways in which we might seek to answer your question. One is again to hold the two of you as models of what Queer people are doing on the planet and how your small steps of unpacking that which has kept you squelched and kept you in grief or guilt or laden with those emotions that will not serve you well. As you have done [that work] you are coming more into that loving disturbance so that wherever you go there is a kind of a disturbance that happens that people are hungry for, especially those who are seekers. They automatical-ly have a recognition that this distur-bance is indeed a loving disturbance, not something to fear or to put a barrier against, but in fact is a source of light.

So what you saw in Hawaii was peo-ple being attracted to your true identities coming through more fully. These identi-ties are emerging as you do your person-al work and are supported by us, your guides and are supported by the ener-getic sparks in you. All of those energetic sparks can help you to raise the level of

"Love is greater than death"
Rev. Elder
Jim Mitulski

your own vibration to higher, more optimal places. We would encourage you to come back to what we said earlier which was BE BOLD BE BOLD BE BOLD [26]

Being Prophetic

The role and function of the prophet is to trust in oneself to speak the truth in love. The offering of such a message requires risk-taking. Soon after these channeling sessions that mentioned the "New Ones", I saw an interview with Jeni Stepanek, the mother of the child poet and peacemaker Mattie Stepanek on Larry King. Mattie was a boy who lived as a peaceful warrior and whose words are prophetic to any age. Mattie faced the challenges of muscular dystrophy until his death at age 13. He began writing poetry at age 3 which seem to break all the boundaries of separation. No matter what Mattie's sexual orientation was or would have been his life depicts the sense I have of what these "New Ones" might be like. Here is a poem Mattie wrote at 8 years old.

On Growing Up (Part 5)

We are growing up

We are many colors of skin

We are many languages

We are many ages and sizes.

We are many countries...

But we are one with the earth.

We each have one heart.

We each have one life

We are growing up, together,

So we must live as one family. [27]

Mattie Stepanek modeled a prophetic life. He seemed to trust that inner voice and risked speak ing his truth in love.

There is a saying/question from the Course in Miracles that is common in 12-step work that asks, "is it better to be right or be free?" Being wrong is not something I enjoy much. First, I don't evaluate the world in right and wrong but in its relevance to balance and energy. Yet, there are clearly times when I "miss the mark." The role and function of the prophet is to trust in oneself to speak the truth in love. The offering of such a message requires risk-taking.

Former Vice President Al Gore in his movie *An Inconvenient Truth* epitomizes the humility of the prophet to go out on a limb to speak the inevitable will happen should we not change our course. Yet such prophecy is reversible if we choose to change our ways.

The potential for queer folk especially to step into more prophetic roles seems likely as we follow an ecstatic path. Yet a conversation I had with a queer associate of Malidoma Somé, a shaman of the African Dagara Tribe shed some light on the dearth of evidence around such prophetic roles. Our musing focused on the role of ancestors in queer wisdom and purpose. In our conversation, Gary Drake, Malidoma's associate, mused with me about the role of ancestors in Queer wisdom and purpose. This brother

spoke of an experience with Malidoma bringing forth words from
the kontomble. (The kontomble are nature spirits, like the Celtic
tradition which calls them fairies).[29] A message came through saying they (the Ancestors) wish to assist us but we must acknowledge
their role with us as Queer folk for that to happen.[30] As we unlayer our karmic stories, body stories and begin remembering
through our bodies who we are as Queer folk, it is my belief our
messages, purposes, gifts and power will be unleashed to heal the
world. Our contribution is necessary to wholeness. As Prophets
and as a prophetic community we must take risks to embody the
Divine in every part of our lives.

As we unlayer our karmic stories and body stories and begin
remembering through our bodies who we are as Queer folk, it is
my belief our messages, purposes, gifts and power will be
unleashed to heal the world. Our contribution is necessary to
wholeness.

As Prophets and as a prophetic community we must take risks
to embody the Divine in every part of our lives.

Archetypes and Our Every Day Lives

This simple, six-personed, six-staged paradigm is best understood as a map of our consciousness. It helps us see who we are and
where we might choose to go with our lives. These archetypes are
like stepping stones on a path. One often leads to another, but the
path is as likely to be a spiral dance as a linear journey. Regardless
of how and when we open ourselves to an inner journey of discovery, these six archetypes invoke powerful, positive images for
Queer people as they heal and build the communities they desire
for themselves.

Historical research confirms that many Queer people have

taken these various roles throughout history. Our ancestors have often been deeply spiritual people on paths of creation and peace-making. We are called to increase social harmony and justice, express our wonder at the beauty of the world, and care for the infirm.

Queer people also seem to have an intrinsic desire to mend dualities in perception, wherever they exist. As the Peaceful Warrior, we strive to mend the rifts between intimacy and detach-ment, unifying power and compassion. As the Lover, flesh and spir-it are one integrated source of delight for us. As the Sacred Prostitute, we invoke the healing power of our erotic bodies, bridg-ing private and individual space with communal, social space. As the Elder, we see no barrier between the many roles we play, uni-fying the "story" of our lives. The Mystic brings pure union with the divine into the physical world, shattering our limiting beliefs. The Prophet delivers the messages of love and change that may come uniquely through the Queer tribe.

It may be a fundamental urge or "calling" for queer people to play such roles as these. Our two-spirited nature leads us to con-front the tyranny of dualistic thinking, to question the borders to limit love in action, and to include others in the delight of a life fully lived. Rumi described "ecstasy" as a boat that was large enough to encompass all of the sorrow and all of the joy of living. Having suffered, having been marginalized, and having prevailed in reclaiming our sexual selves against all odds, we are capable of living authentic, ecstatic lives as Rumi charges us to. The practice of such a life is not divorced from the nitty-gritty of the workaday world; instead, such a practice embraces every aspect of life, free-ing us in the process.

Reclaiming Ancient Wisdom:

Visual renderings of archetypal awareness can help us see the essential unity of our consciousness. These three very useful renderings (and related images) are shown to illustrate the archetypes.

Ecstatic Journey: a personal journey of growth and world change

In the first model, we see the path through the archetypes as a linear journey.

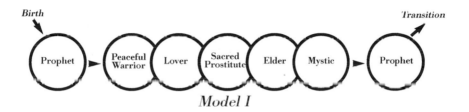

Model I

Medicine Wheels, Mandalas, and the Activation of the Five Elements

In the second model, the first four major archetypes (or four directions in a circle) articulate as turning points on a wheel of consciousness. This model draws inspiration from the "medicine wheel". The center (fifth) pulls in the integrated energy of all directions and pulsates them out as the Mystic aligns him/herself with the source. Each archetype and direction is also associated with one of the four elements: earth, air, fire and water. Woven together, the four archetypes, directions and elements recreate the life cycle of our planet. The Prophet encircles the journey. The activating archetype, it propels into being the beginning (and continuum) through the end of this embodied journey.

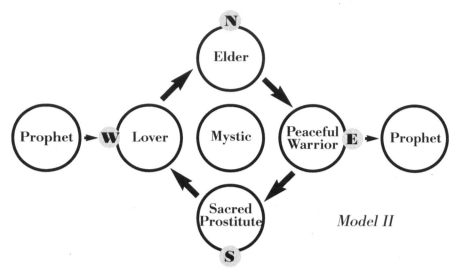

Model II

Transforming the Emotion and Energy of Body Stories

The third model relates the medicine wheel of archetypes to the emotional challenges associated with each archetype. Each archetype in this medicine wheel contains an integration of all elements, for these archetypes are emerging again in our culture (especially queer culture) because it is "time." The need for archetypes that usher in the new world of hope and promise is an aspect of this medicine wheel. All elements are necessary for this alchemical effect,

On this wheel the East is the place of new beginnings, a dawn, a journey from the outer world to the inner world of the west. The Peaceful warrior starts the journey deeply listening to the heart of the Mother, earth, to face the beasts of fear to become the beauty. The archetypes on the wheel are essential for the change agent (the Peaceful Warrior) to know him/herself. The heartful warrior may step out of the traditional path going forth and cross to the inner flow of water in the West. Discovering in the innermost place of the setting sun, the Lover, wishes to unite polarities within him/herself. The Lover flows emotion, magic and grief. Rumi says, "the agony of lovers is the doorway to God." Seeing the face of the beloved in all is the intimate work of the lover. Often the peaceful warriors journey goes South (especially for queer men) exploring the heat, fire and passion of the Sacred Prostitute. If the sojourner comes as the peaceful warrior, willing to face his/her fears, shame is transformed with the recognition of the erotic and spiri-

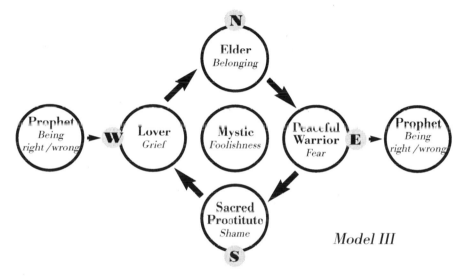

Model III

tual being one and sexual expression as gift. No matter how the journey proceeds for the warrior of spirit his/her work must embody both the lover and sacred prostitute to be initiated as Elder. Among indigenous peoples, the North is often considered the place of the elders' wisdom. The queer peaceful warrior often comes out as a same sex lover and erotic healer into a depth of wisdom held by the elders of the tribe. It is this integrated wisdom that honors all paths. In the North the element of air, breathes the ancestral knowledge to all who would listen and learn.

At the center of this journey of ecstasy, where the earth and sky meet, is the Mystic. The merger, the union with the energies of the Divine is where one finds him/herself living more and more. The element guiding the Mystic is light. The radiance of all the wisdom the new warrior has gathered is now in perfect alignment. Here a vision of wholeness is experienced for moments, hours, days and on, as the prophet's message is re-awakened. The Prophet, who is the nature of the Queer person from birth, has gone the journey of the Peaceful Warrior, Lover, Sacred Prostitute, Elder and Mystic, ready to speak a new consciousness of love. As a communicator of truth, The Prophet is guided by the element/vibration of sound.

Symbolic Maps

The model I'm presenting seems subliminal in many traditional images. These images and symbols speak to our intuition and unconscious mind. These symbols seem to "call forth" the ancestors and invoke ritual work that has been developed in many global cultures. For example, Leonardo da Vinci's "Vitruvian Man" is a fascinating and very popular image. The four limbs and head of the man create a five-pointed star within a circle. In the diagram shown, each point includes the embodiment of all five archetypes.

Among the Iroquois Nation, the Asskouandy (at left) is another diagram of the five fold path held in a circle that is both mystical and transformative.

The pentagram, used by pantheistic and earth-oriented religions like Wicca was also used by early Christians. As such, it has a long history as a life-affirming, positive symbol. Like many images of healing and integration, it was later depicted as Satanic and was used to oppress witches and healers who practiced outside of officially sanctioned Christian organizations. Many queer people find themselves drawn to this symbol, and reclaim it for the healing symbol that it is.

Body / Earth Wisdom and Direct Experience

It is worth noting that when indigenous peoples utilize paradigms like the medicine wheel to describe their spiritual identity, they are striving for an integrated awareness of body, mind and spirit. This runs counter to the general scientific mindset that governs Western thinking. For example, the Periodic Table of Elements defines many unique substances, but our exploration of the spiritual essence of "elements" need not be so exact to be useful. Indeed, "modern" societies depend heavily on the exercise of "critical thinking," but all too often, we disregard the experience and wisdom of the body. The absence of mystery and spirit in our popular culture symbolizes the poverty of science as the sole descriptor of the world around us.

Discernment

The ecstatic explorations, techniques and processes in this book come from stories of our remembering. Remembering who we are, remembering our connection to the earth, source and each other and our remembering of our mission, purpose or essence.

Experiential work and altered states open us to a wealth of information. Data from visions, dreams, impressions, feelings, emotions and sensations experienced in the body are subject to many interpretations and analyses. These experiences enrich our lives with guidance, meaning and wisdom, yet discernment is necessary for a mature ecstatic path.

It seems reasonable the ask the question, "from whence does this information come?" Identifying the source for the vision, dream or impression may assist in discerning its meaning and relevance. When gatekeepers from the Dagara tribe go into caves, or when Native American shamans enter a sweat lodge, they know the kinds of spirits that might speak to them. In such ceremonies of ecstasy, the sources of Spirit are externalized but integrated internally.

Ecstatic work, however, often awakens wisdom from within the body itself. In the tissues, fluids, bones, or the very DNA, the information of remembering seems to be drawn out. One pertinent question here is whether the remembering is appearing from a wounded body story (from this lifetime or another) or from the story of one's wholeness/essence.

Where this information originated, as well as how to use the information offered, frames the discernment process for the erotic spiritual aspirant.

Through years of facilitating Erotic Body Prayer, many phenomenological experiences have happened. How the celebrants used the information they received causes me to underscore the need for discernment.

I have often found that a wounded body story and a whole body story may surface simultaneously thus making the information brought forth seem confusing or dismissible.

During an erotic body prayer session, a brother had a vision of himself moving from San Francisco to another city and working as a healer. He immediately acted on this vision even though it seemed ungrounded to me. In this new city, it became evident the move was a flight from dealing with some past relationships. However, in the awareness he also discovered that his work as a healer was clearly his path. He returned to San Francisco and found his healing practice flowed with ease. This overlapping "remembering" from a wounded body story (to flee when conflict appears) and a whole story, remembering his essence as a healer, emerged together. When they were recognized separately, the truth from each part of the revelation brought freedom.

Discerning body wisdom has some almost obvious criteria. The process and the results are freedom, wholeness, you, peace, harmony and, of course, love. Wisdom may often feel uncomfortable at first. However, it should always lead to a higher plane.

The proclamation, "You shall know them by their fruits" is a saying attributed to Jesus. It is an underlying criterion of discernment. What is produced inside a person and what it manifests outside in one's world is the test of the Spirit from which it comes.

Ecstatic work naturally moves blood, oxygen, nutrients and energy through the body creating an atmosphere for subjective impressions to awaken through the body. These subjective experiences may produce faith, not from an absolute certainty but form opening the hunger to keep searching and seeking. Possibly the greatest criterion then for discernment is not to have an answer but "to live in the question" as the propellant for the ecstatic pursuant.

The body's wisdom continues to reveal itself in languages like the medicine wheel. The elements are present, yet the mystery is

71

ever being revealed

III. Kirk's Personal Journey

My own experience with the "Elements" deepened while working on the initial Erotic Body Prayer Manual. I spent a week at Kalani Honua, a retreat center near Kilauea Volcano on the Island of Hawaii. One evening several guests at the retreat center went together to pay respects to Pel'e, the goddess of the volcano. Pel'e's house is located at Kilauea Crater, which has been very active in recent years, pouring lava directly into the Pacific Ocean.

As we walked over the hardened lava to get to the site where we would watch the volcano speak out her presence, I was aware of being altered in mind and body. The first sight of the volcano's fire spewing into the ocean waves, steam rising high into the sky, moved me into a place of no words. Before me was a visual, felt experience of the cycle of life. Her magic of creation moved deep into my body. The medicine wheel was being displayed in the synthesis of all four elements.

Our paths as queer men are diverse, encompassing different ethnic communities and histories. But the archetypal cycle described in Erotic Body Prayer may be regarded as a path, with markers for us to relate to on our journey. These archetypes are ancient, yet they exist in dynamic harmony with new images for us to see ourselves living out our greatest potential. Like Pel'e, the elements combined to form and embody a gift of magic.

The Caldron

In the summer of 1989 I attended my third AIDS Medicine and Miracles Conference in Boulder, Colorado. I had been going every year to learn more about the interplay between traditional and complimentary holistic healing methods for HIV. At the closing of the conference, an open mike was available to the audience for personal remarks. My friend and soul-mate, Wayne, approached the microphone and concisely said, "I came here a person with AIDS and I am leaving a person." Along with Wayne and several colleagues, I had been working on an article titled "A Healing Journey for the HIV Challenged Person." Wayne's statement epitomized the heart of our article. By doing integrated body and soul work at the conference, Wayne reclaimed his power one more time, and asserted his right to dissociate himself from disease and the many negative connotations that were attached to it. I was very proud of him.

Following the conference, around 30 people decided to create a sweat lodge to extend the experience of closing into focused gratitude and prayer. This was my first experience of a Native American-style sweat lodge. Like any first experience, it was laced with excitement, anticipation and anxiety.

I had been intimately involved with a number of people going to the sweat lodge, which included both men and women. But I had never been naked with them, sweating and praying in a consecrated and sacred place. By this point in my spiritual journey I had become very well-versed in the erotic spirituality work that was pioneered by elders like Joseph Kramer, John Ballew, and James Broughton. Being naked across genders and sexual orientations, combined with the physical experience of sweating and praying, revealed profound new levels of awareness for me.

My recollection of the experience is highlighted with "snapshot" moments that will forever be held in memory. I sat in the dark cave, which felt like the very womb of the earth, the ledge of our spirits. I recall the invocations to the four directions, an open invitation to call forth spirit within us. Wayne and I sat far in the back of the circle of darkness, under the pall of steam and heat. Every so often sparks would fly from the sweetgrass being scattered on the scorching rocks, illuminating the brothers and sisters around us. As lodge leaders poured more water on the scalding rocks, the steam became almost overwhelming. Bending low to the earth, I tried to find more breath to take into my energized body. At one point the energetic sensations in my body tingled with the sense of indwelling spirits, friends who had passed. Somewhere between chanting, laughing and crying, I heard Wayne improvising a song to himself. "You are beautiful baby," he sang, "you are so beautiful." "You will be all right." My body ached, as it strained for oxygen and yet I was total delighted at the same time.

Several years later, Wayne died, a warrior in his own right. Afterwards I had an opportunity to attend another sweat lodge in North Carolina. The guide for this gathering was a native man named Peter Bear Walks. Peter took us through the complete process of creating the sweat lodge, as it comes from the Native American tradition. The group consisted of twenty gay and bisexual men. Each man participated in the building of the lodge. The gathering process involved approaching the stones, the trees and shrubs of the surrounding land and asking them if they wished to be a part of this lodge. This process of reverence for of the elements of the lodge awakened my body and soul to hear what the rocks and trees might say. Once again, the sweat lodge experience took me to a deep place of reverence for my connection to all things.

In this second sweat lodge, my experience flowed quickly from one level of awareness into the next. Throughout the ritual I was filled with a sense of the sacred. While I was in the lodge, with its energetic ritual, steam, flesh, sweat, and invocations, in visions I witnessed my mother, my father, Wayne and many other people who had died. As they floated through my consciousness, I felt their presence within the fabric of my body. I recall a flash of insight, telling me that all of me was praying-not only my mind or heart, but every pore of my body, in a single integrated energy flow. I felt connected to the earth, the sweat, the men and the energies of people, places and things across time.

Coming to San Francisco

This was many years ago. Since then, I have moved to San Francisco. As I began to sink new roots into the community, I identified several places and fellowships that I wanted to be part of. Some were very simple. For example, I made a point of having breakfast every day at Orphan Andy's, a restaurant in the Castro District.

I also started attending the Metropolitan Community Church of San Francisco (MCC-SF). MCC-SF sponsors a Wednesday night service called "Prayer of the Heart". The service is patterned after those popularized at Taizé, a French religious community that expresses prayer through song, words and periods of silence. Whenever I attend the MCC-SF Taizé services, I experience a warm sensation in my body, a softening of the heart that is very comforting. However, I also become keenly aware of more difficult feelings, like grief or pain. During the service, people are invited to kneel or stand at a candle lit cross in the center of the room. As people quietly approach the center of the room to pray, the encircling congregation continues singing songs or saying chants, over and over. On the first occasion that I went to kneel in the center of the circle while the others sang, I was aware of a unique blend of unconditional love and acceptance, a feeling so great that the encompassed all of the sorrows or loss that I felt in my life. It was as though my body was enfolded in a womb, surrounded by fluid intentions and infinite potential. The vastness of connection and joy was strikingly reminiscent of my experience in sweat lodges.

These powerful sensations are not new feelings for me, but they are connected to my own path of healing. I am aware that I have the same inner awakening almost every time I exchange touch. This fundamental openness of spirit is always part of my lovemaking. It is out of this "body wisdom" that I have created the process called Erotic Body Prayer. It is related to the wisdom that the twelfth century mystic poet Rumi expressed when he said, "If you ask me how Jesus raised the dead. Kiss me on the lips."[2] The sensations of a lover expressing his/her spirit passionately, through the body and with an open heart, raises up new life. It is the process of erotic body prayer, and it is available to anyone who wishes to

live mindfully in the fullness of their erotic body.

My history of spiritual exploration has involved a conscious commitment to integrate erotic energy into the healing process. As a sexual healer, I have witnessed healing and transformation in people of every sort. I have seen bodies and souls change both gradually and instantaneously. It is my belief that as we embrace who we are more fully, we are able to manifest our gifts for healing ourselves much more clearly. Using prayer, and redefining prayer is a key for many of us to move more fully into our gifts. Some of us have come to this awareness through experiences like sweat lodges, or Taoist/Tantric erotic massage—forms of prayer that encompass body and spirit. Such forms give expression to moments when all of our being is present and participating. Erotic Body Prayer is another method of prayer through the body that calls us to "be there": to be fully present to the messages we receive not only from the body, but from every part of us.

IV. Erotic Body Prayer: The Basic Philosophy

Simply stated, Erotic Body Prayer processes are pathways for praying through the body. The process embraces ancient wisdom and archetypes, along with ideas from psychics and energy medicine. Erotic Body Prayer provides a method of exploring healing through the integration of the erotic and spiritual. Erotic Body Prayer invites the celebrants into greater maturity and consciousness as they touch and transform themselves, and thus each other. Many of the techniques that are used will be familiar to those who have been involved in various types of bodywork: verbalized intentions, energy work, breath, sound ritual, posturing, boundary setting, safe erotic play and so on. Together, these processes guide the celebrants through a process of being more available to each other. As they do so, they become more open to healing, pleasure and intimacy. The actual process of Erotic Body Prayer may vary, depending on the needs of the individual, couple or group. The essence, however is constant, and is best expressed through two repeated questions: "What do you want to heal?" and "How/where do you want to send this energy we are raising?"

As one moves through the process of sensing energy without touch, then with very light touch, and finally with erotic play, the above questions are asked repeatedly. As energy moves, one becomes increasingly altered. The questions begin to solicit responses from the unconscious mind and from body memory (body stories). Stating what one wants to heal or how to direct the energy being raised becomes a prayer, an agreement, an intention carried with the energy being shared.

Prayer

In developing the basic philosophy of Erotic Body Prayer, I wish to reclaim and broaden the scope of the word "prayer." One of my mystery school teachers is a contemporary mystic named Ron Roth, currently called Sri Ronji. My history with Sri Ronji began around 1986. I first heard his name, Ron Roth, while I was meditating. I had never heard of him before, so I wrote it down on a piece of paper and put it aside. Weeks later, I received a brochure in my psychotherapy office about a workshop on archetypes by Caroline Myss. Whose name was also on the brochure? Ron Roth, of course. I attended the workshop with Caroline where Ron made a guest appearance to lead a healing meditation. In that first experience of Ron, I was not impressed. Since then,however, I now hold him as a significant guide on my spiritual journey.

One repetitive teaching Sri Ronji speaks of is about defining prayer.[1] Sri Ronji taught one definition for the word "prayer" as "pal al" from the Sanskrit writings meaning "seeing yourself as wondrously made." This is an affirmation I use in my work, especially in creating safe and sacred space for erotic touch. Participants are guided to say to each other, "You are wondrously made." Sri Ronji also shared the word for prayer in Aramaic (the language Jesus used) as "slotha". When Jesus spoke what is typically called The Lord's Prayer, he said, "When you pray, pray like this." The Aramaic word "slotha." means "to set (your mind as) a trap," to catch the thoughts of God. Sri Ronji says, "I've come to see that prayer isn't about our words or thoughts. It's about the realization of oneness with God and all creation. "What we hold in that trap is our interconnectedness."[2]

The journey of erotic spiritual work contains at its core these two intentions. To pray, knowing that everyBODY despite shape, form, color, sex/gender, orientation, functional wholeness and disease or wellness status is "wondrously made" along with knowing, in the trap of one's mind that the phrase "We Are One" is central to ecstasy and prayer. I imagine the ancient sacred prostitutes held these two intentions as they brought their bodies to serve Goddess/God and their celebrant in rituals of healing.

A thousand years after the temples of the sacred prostitutes were

This icon of Mary Magdalene by Robert Lentz was produced for Grace Cathedral San Francisco.

squelched or destroyed, a mythic vestige of the archetype resurfaces in the Christian literature. One of the Marys breaks a vase of oil to pour over the Christ's feet. She is depicted sensuously spreading the oil using her hair. I recognize this archetypal act as that of an erotic healer praying with her body and her heart, giving Christ (the annointed one) an offering of pleasure.

Several Kinds of Prayer

Accentuating Sri Ronji's teaching of holding intention (or setting the trap of oneness and highest potential), I would refer also to the research of Larry Dossey, M.D. I heard Dr. Dossey speak about the research of using prayer for healing.[3] The researchers used groups of people who would pray for those (whom they did not know) around their physical disease processes. When looking at two kinds of prayers offered by groups towards subjects, their findings indicated the groups that prayed with specific intentions like "get rid of this cancer" had less evidence of change than the group whose prayer was like holding the subject in love and light or Well-Being. Erotic Body Prayer is the use of ecstatic states to propel a similar intention for the highest good. As we consider the rich body of research and analog material that teaches us of healing, it is always my desire to offer as many personal truths as may be found on a given subject. While conducting an erotic body prayer session, specific themes, images or self-statements may emerge that allow one to set a more direct and clear intention than that implied in the Larry Dossey studies. "Body stories" may emerge in the process of the ecstatic exchange that becomes a direct prayer. Feelings, sensations and word clusters may show up around body image, sexual performance or function, religious shame or guilt, pleasure, and being witnessed erotically. "Nasty," "dirty," "prohibited," and "unacceptable" are words and stories of judgment that the gift of pleasure may heal, when one realizes the erotic and spiritual are one.

An example of this happened while I was working with a man who was very overweight for his height. As we began some massage and ecstatic breathwork, it was clear to both of us he felt great shame about his body form. A simple acknowledgement of that shame allowed him to be more present. Using erotic touch in the massage with him, he seemed to lighten up, almost physically to my perception. As I closed the session, I did a Reiki treatment on him in which I felt pain and pressure in my left ear. I asked him, "Do you have an earache?" "Yes," he said, "how do you know that?" I replied, "Well, I often feel things in my body where the energy is going in yours, thus I felt an ache in my ear." "Wow," he said. So in this instance it was clear to me I had been given some information that his ear was ready for healing. So I asked him to imagine the earache leaving as I simply spoke softly, "Earache leave. Be whole." The intention here was very specific for physical healing. It was my belief he became available to the physical healing after the emotional healing around the body head been released. His earache was gone and so was some of his shame. Sri Ronji speaks of mystics like Jesus never using prayer as pleading for something, but as a decree. There are times when it is clear that the healer is not interfering with the client's life but acting in accordance with the client's desire to heal body stories and embrace a full physical/spiritual manifestation. Each person's soul journey influences when or how the healing manifests. In these cases you are not really stepping out on a limb by affirming their truth. Concluding some ideas on the nature of prayer, I recognize it is often a process. I did some work with Elizabeth Kübler-Ross before she died. She spoke of marinating people in the energy of prayer. Whenever possible," touch people as you marinate them in love," she said.[4] She loved working with babies, especially babies born with HIV. Marinating the babies in love often had miraculous results.

Throughout my life, I have been privileged to work with many healers and shamans from many traditions. Often through the energetic presence of the healer, a decree or a ritual, I have seen miracles take place. And what I also know from these practitioners is that a cancer, a pain, a circumstance may be relieved, but if the subject does not do his own psychological, emotional, spiritual, and body-story work, the ailment will reappear.

Pleasuring Prayer

Pleasuring prayer encompasses all these ideas and consists of simply charging our bodies while setting an intention. Pleasure raises the energy to set in motion the intention in our hearts. Pleasuring prayer also may allow us to re-wire some of the old stories in our bodies weaving all these concepts together. Pleasure is a moment in which we experience wholeness. Although the old stories may emerge in response to pleasure as some form of judgment, in the actual moment of pleasure there are no stories of shut downs, numbness, or sabotage. This is Truly a Holy moment for it is a glimpse of wholeness. As we touch ourselves and each other we affirm "You are wondrously made. I am wondrously made." An intention is held and propelled to the universe with pleasure.

Flesh & Spirit Community began an experiment called 'Pleasuring Prayer" as part of our regular rituals. Body stories about the separation of the erotic from the spiritual surfaced as the circle set an intention (around a concern) and then used guided methods of self pleasure or interactive pleasure to propels this intention energetically out to the Universe. This concept is huge when one gets concrete. One brother set an intention for a family member's healing and then we began our self pleasuring exercises to raise the energy on her behalf. The gap between religious training, witnessed genital touch and prayer brought clarity
to the residual stories of disconnection. Healing often starts with naming the story. It takes a peaceful warrior spirit to to be willing to know oneself that fully.

The subtle difference between Erotic Body Prayer and Pleasuring Prayer is the attention to pleasure. Erotic Body Prayer involves all the methods and practices written in this book, of which, Pleasuring Prayer is just one expression.

There are many topics from first century Christian writings of Paul that have wounded, defamed and alienated many from the inclusive message of love. However, his admonition to "pray without ceasing" is one I fully embrace. Prayer is about how we live, move and have our being and especially as queer folk how we step into our divine authority as erotic spiritual guardians. As the basic philosophy of erotic body prayer is fleshed out, reclaim these words "pray without ceasing"

Basic Philosophy

The essential aspects of Erotic Body Prayer might be sewn together with two major threads: the thread from the growing body of literature found on surviving and thriving in one's body; and the thread emerging from the term, "midwife of the dying."

Surviving and thriving literature has been expounded upon throughout this book and may be accessed under titles of behavioral medicine, complimentary medicine, holistic health, energy medicine, long term survivorship, hardiness studies and psychoneuroimmunology. Numerous researchers, helping professionals and participants in the research of these studies have been Queer in nature. One such pioneer was Dr. George Solomon, whose research produced the term psychoneuroimmunology to describe the link between the mind, emotions and body.[5] Looking at diseases such as rheumatoid arthritis and AIDS, Dr. Solomon discovered some loose themes that characterize persons living longer and better in their bodies through "dis-ease" processes. Dr. Solomon's work and the work of Dr. Candace Pert[6] have been significant in developing the models contained within Erotic Body Prayer.

The long term survivor literature has brought us back to a

deep listening to our bodies and a full celebration of being at home in our bodies. Alongside this knowledge of living fully in the experience of our body is the knowledge we are more than our body.

Deepak Chopra speaks of cancer survivors and those experiencing spontaneous healings often being people who hold the notion that they are more than just their bodies.[7]

During the first decade of AIDS, my work was strongly focused on supporting people to "live with AIDS" and many did, and still do. However, I have been personally involved with the lives of around three hundred people who died. I was able to participate directly in some of these transitions, while I became aware of other's deaths after the exit from the body had occurred.

Some of these passings, transitions or deaths seemingly were "good deaths" and others "bad deaths" from the eyes of one on the physical plane, yet all of them opened a river in my heart that will never be closed. Being able to play the intimate and sacred role of midwife to the dying, a role I believe all Queer folk may play, was a gift. To help someone cross the threshhold between life and death is to walk between worlds, to occupy the special niche that Queer people occupy as soon as they sense their difference.

Care-giving is a common attribute among many Queer people. Creative ways of offering help and service to one in need from the beginning of one's life to the end of life can be seen among all tribes. Yet, often the LGBT (Lesbian, gay, bisexual and transgendered) community expresses care-giving with a unique face and with unique expressions.

I have only been present at one birth in my life so far. As I stood watching this miracle take shape before me, I recall the sensations in my body. The same sensations as when I have prayed ecstatically, or when I watch a volcano pour forth lava or even when I have made love were streaming through my body. My recollection of that birth is the memory of a glorious sunrise.

Equally powerful and amazingly similar, of course, is the privilege of holding the hand (literally or energetically) of someone who is about to make their final exit. "Midwiving the dying" is a developing term being used by healing communities and helping care professionals to describe the multiple facets of participating in the life transition. In the work of Erotic Body Prayer, the midwife of the dying facilitates an ecstatic environment for healing into life or death.

The six major archetypes described in this book (Peaceful Warrior, Lover, Sacred Prostitute, Elder, Mystic and Prophet) are all facilitators of ecstasy and create a bridge to another world. Thus, each of these archetypes demonstrates the action of being a midwife of the dying.

The philosophy, then, of Erotic Body Prayer speaks to the inner journey of being fully alive in one's body and the wisdom that we are more than just our bodies on a journey of wholeness. These two threads weave the backdrop for this erotic spiritual journey.

The basic tenets of Erotic Body Prayer are:

A. Energy emanates inside and outside the body.

B. Thought, breath, movement, sound and posturing cause psychological, neurological and energetic changes in and around the physical body.

C. To the degree that all aspects of the self are in agreement (prayer) the creative force of our being becomes active to influence our lives. As all aspects of the body and soul agree, a sense of presence and aliveness increases.

D. Combining and weaving energies from sources outside (i.e., the universal "Chi") and our energy heightens the potential for healing. These shared energies help to reveal the truth of our experience so we can choose more wholeness.

E. The body is a store house of memory and experience. All the pain, ecstasy, and other strong emotions have been registered in the body. The ways in which these experiences have been held in the body may influence our wellness. These body stories are located both in the cellular and energetic body.

F. Although the outcomes to weaving our energies together (prayer) may be amazing, both client and practitioners must stay free from attachments. This allows them to be fully present to whatever moment of healing may occur, however mysterious its emergence may be at the onset.

V. Healing Stories and Therapeutic Practice

The very process of touching others bodies consciously and intentionally provides healing. As practitioners and clients discover the flow of energy within the body, the potential healing power of intentional touch is vastly increased. Many men have reported feeling more alive, present and available to receive pleasure after having participated in an Erotic Body Prayer session.

The healing energy of Erotic Body Prayer may also lead to unexpected breakthroughs. For example, although Erotic Body Prayer is not focused on grief or loss, many men experience closure in grieving processes. When closure is achieved they find that they are more available for intimate relationships. In some cases, men have experienced physical healing. However, Erotic Body Prayer is not focused on linear outcomes. Instead it is focused on creating more wholeness and joy in the areas that the client desires to work on and heal.

The most common response of queer men who have done several erotic body prayer sessions has been the dissolving of grief due to losses of intimacy, broken relationships, death (especially AIDS losses), sickness and fatigue from perceived rejections.

Your effulgence has lit a fire in my heart and you

have made radiant for me the earth and the sky.

My arrow of love has arrived at the target. I am in

the house of mercy and my heart has

a place of prayer.[1]

Rumi

Therapeutic Stories From My Bodywork Practice

The following examples are derived from my bodywork practice. Most names have been altered to retain confidentiality except the first two, who gave full disclosure and wrote their own stories.

I have facilitated hundreds of Erotic Body Prayer sessions with queer men. I have also trained numerous men to put to use what they have learned in their relationships. Many have reported dynamic changes and shifts in their lives. Sometimes these changes are subtle, but they can be sudden and profound. The following vignettes are true stories with minor alterations to maintain the confidences of the client.

Jim Stratton (by Jim Stratton)

My recovery process has included recovering from many addictions. The first was alcohol/drugs and last but perhaps most pervasive was sex. The pleasure and energy from the use of sex was one of my earliest discoveries but the recovery from the compulsive, deadening, unconscious use of sex was the last and the most difficult to be healed.. After many years in recovery in 12-step programs. I abstained from any form of sexuality. Once I learned to be abstinent it was easy not to be sexual when I wanted to become sexual again. I was overcome with fear and trepidation. I had no idea how to recover my erotic/sexual self. I was afraid that if were sexual I would return to compulsive, destructive behaviors. Flesh and Spirit Community, Erotic Body Prayer work has been where I have learned how to use and follow my sexual energy–to explore the sacred/sexual connection. For years I believed my erotic self was separate from my spiritual self. One of my most frightening early experiences was to be in a room of naked, erotic, gay men and to be present. My experience in F & S gave me back the choice about where, when and how I am erotic. In this work I had a powerful experience of a "full body climax" with seeing Jesus present. I now have been able to combine my Christian roots with my sexual life. The first time I experienced an ecstatic massage was the first time I knew I could pursue pleasure just for purpose of pleasure. My body came alive, turned on, and was stimulated. For me addiction was a journey away from self–which contributed to a compulsive drive. Healing has been to reconnect my erotic/sexual/spiritual energies into one. Discovering they are all one has been a journey back to self.

Matty Johnson (by Matty Johnson)

Eight years ago I ended up in rehab. After over a decade of alcoholism, my life was in shambles and I felt invisible. I was uncomfortable in my own body and disconnected with my sexuality. I felt like an imposter, like I did not measure up as a "real" gay man. I felt isolated from the gay community and was buried in shame. I was in a spiritual void with no sense of purpose or direction. I did not like the person I was. Luckily I found Kirk Prine, and my work with Flesh & Spirit has completely transformed my life.

Today I am an ardent gym rat, and have numerous tattoos. This year I earned a place on the SOMA Bare Chest Calendar, and competed for and won a leather title. I am no longer invisible: I want

2006 Rich Stadtmiller www.RichTrove.com

to be seen and to be part of the community around me. Four years ago I met a wonderful man —and I surprised myself by being both emotionally and physically available for a relationship with him. Today we are domestic partners. I just received tenure in the CSU, and am enjoying my career as a professor. I like the person I now am. I am tremendously grateful to Kirk Prine and my brothers in Flesh & Spirit for supporting my transformation. I now feel at home at in my body.

Tim

Tim lost his partner of thirteen years to AIDS. Although he had occasional sexual partners, he never felt fully connected to himself in the experience. He also felt limited in his ability to emotionally connect with the man he was sharing his body with. In Erotic Body Prayer sessions, Tim discovered a well of grief and sorrow within him than he had blocked from his awareness. The more Tim listened to his body as we focused on intentional erotic touch and energy flows in his body, the more he would cry. His tears felt like they were touching something deep inside, yet the specific source of grief was never fully clear.

As we would pause, allowing Tim the time to name his intention—his prayer—he would just say repeatedly the word, "Available." "I want to be available," he sighed. After each session Tim would talk about the process and how he felt more alive in his body, more open to spirit and to himself.

My work with Tim was ongoing for years. We met regularly for sessions that continued to feel transformational. Then, one day I became aware I had not from Tim for a month. Shortly after that, I met him by chance in the Castro, and shared my concern about not seeing him. He was spilling over with joy about having met a man who he loved, and could allow into his heart and body. This was the first time outside of our sessions he had felt this way since his lover died. A year later, I heard from Tim again. This time he expressed deep gratitude for the work he did with me. It was clear to him that his conscious work to heal had enabled him to be available for a meaningful relationship. The very act of expressing gratitude to me was symbolic of the deep healing that Tim had experienced, and is strong evidence of the two-way healing process that Erotic Body Prayer encompasses.

Michael

Michael was another peaceful warrior who had suffered deeply during the HIV epidemic. In one Erotic Body Prayer session, he recovered a memory of the death of his partner. He had held his partner in his arms until his death—a powerful experience that has been shared by many queer men. He simply used the session to heal his pain of separation. The sessions gave back to Michael the love and support that he had given to his dying partner. Since his work in Erotic Body Prayer Michael has taken much better care of himself. His body and his health became more dynamic since he let go of what he no longer needed.

Ivan

Ivan came to me to work on his history as a sexual abuse survivor. The process involved moving slowly with intentional touch, using only thoughts and energy to teach comfort and healing to Ivan. As he felt safer, he took his power back by asking for what he wanted and the ways he wanted to be touched.

It was clear that Ivan needed to disassociate the pleasure of healthy sexuality from the pain and humiliation of sexual abuse. As we introduced moments of erotic pleasure that were entirely free of pain or emotional abuse, we focused our energy—our prayers—toward the queer boy who had been abused. Tears, laughter, passion and calmness emerged as wonderful by products of the work Ivan did for himself.

Harry

Harry experienced ambivalent, confusing messages from his body that blocked his ability to enjoy sex, and he set an intention to understand why this was so. During a session we opened up his body with intentional touch, and then moved into cock play. He quickly noted some discomfort in his cock. We began a direct dialogue with his cock, naming his genitalia as a location where blockage was stored. As we expanded the dialogue with his cock, it became increasingly clear that we could engage in breath work to open up his erotic body.

As we breathed, Harry seemed to have an actual rebirth experience that evoked old feelings of not being wanted, and more specifically, the trauma and pain of circumcision. The pathway of healing for Harry was to love the inner child that had been so misunderstood and unsupported. As the breath work progressed, Harry, who was a massive and muscular man, became very soft like a baby. In the safety of Erotic Body Prayer this "rugged" man could begin to learn how to nurture the playful inner child, which can melt away the wounds and burdens of our lives with innocence and unconditional self-love.

Javier

Javier was a very evolved man who had come to learn more about his own life journey. He had done much grief work in the past, and he just wanted to be more alive and available for healing others. After several deeply connected sessions, Javier found that he was more able to connect to men who had died and left him. This alone seemed profound. Yet as we continued our Erotic Body Prayer sessions, the energy between us seemed to raise powerfully. Soon we reached ecstatic states that were reminiscent of Pentecost, the indwelling of Spirit. It is common through in Pentecostal revival meetings to be "slain in the spirit:" to fall over and feel energy coursing through the body. Javier would fall back and shake with ecstatic joy. It is extremely significant that intentional body work like Erotic Body Prayer can enable queer men to create authentic, spiritual experiences simply by awakening the body; Javier's openness to unity of body and mind were immensely enriching for him. As a practitioner, witnessing and participating in such life-changing work is an honor and a privilege.

Tom

Tom was a man living with cancer. He was undergoing radiation treatments for cancer and found that his own body had become a stranger to him. He reached out to many for help. He used Erotic Body Prayer sessions to help minimize the side effects for his treatment, escalate healing and stay erotically available. Most people who undergo cancer treatment "shut down" their erotic bodies, which can deny the healing power of pleasure as part of the healing process. Tom was wise to choose to nurture all that he could in his erotic body. I am certain that it has been a vital part of his remission from cancer.

Frank

Frank came to do Erotic Body Prayer sessions because he felt generally inadequate and unattractive. Ironically, he was both physically and emotionally beautiful, yet he felt small and damaged. Frank utilized sessions to connect to his body from the inside out. He gave himself complete freedom to "act out" extreme emotions in a safe space, crying, screaming and laughing. As he did so, the signs of energy—prayer—became ever more apparent. He used his sessions to begin to heal the schism between his external beauty and his inner beauty, to unlearn all of the messages that our society uses to put beauty on a pedestal—which can be a very lonely place. He began to rediscover the small boy inside that he so longed to love, but had never learned how. His experiential body-work became a gateway to integrating very practical life skills that have enabled him to be happier and more fulfilled. The boy was the gateway to a new life for Frank, because its messages of love were simple, powerful and transformational.

VI. Simple Steps for Erotic Body Prayer

The following steps, processes and personal history provide a framework for practitioners and others who are interested in creating their own experiences with Erotic Body Prayer.

These steps may be used as a methodological process or any one step may be the focus of the ecstatic work. The themes from the archetypes, The Peaceful Warrior, the Lover, The Sacred Prostitute, The Elder, The Mystic and The Prophet are embodied in these ideas, practices, techniques and tools. It is not being suggested one embrace each of these methods as a vehicle to ecstacy or that each environmental condition must be in place for magic to happen. In the palm of your hand is a spectrum of opportunities.

A. Creating a Sacred Space

For bodywork to take on its full potential for healing, it needs be approached with reverence. This begins with the physical location where the bodywork takes place. The physical environment can be planned to reflect the reverence and sacredness of the practitioner's intentions to offer healing, and a calm, safe space to the client.

Creating a sacred space starts and ends with intention: intention to welcome yourself and your client, but also to welcome any guides or spiritual sources as you understand them. The practitioner may exercise creativity in using tools that will connect the bodywork with ritual, traditions of love, symbols of meaning, and archetypes of consciousness. The conscious intention to use imagery and objects that send positive message sets the tone for the journey, and for the surprises it may give birth to.

Setting intention can be a simple as the lighting of a candle, or saying a prayer like "I put myself in love and light, no harm can come from me and no harm can come to me."

As queer men, we have well-developed talents for creating an environment of beauty. Take the time necessary to develop rituals that honor the link between flesh and spirit.

Simple actions of purification and healing can have a profound, positive influence on erotic life. For example, after I first moved to San Francisco, I would make regular visits to Eros, a sex club. My intention was to use these visits to balance my own energy, since my daily role as a sexual healer demanded considerable energy and great attention on my part as a caregiver.

During these visits, I noticed there were some occasions when my connections to men were deeper and more amazing than other times. I came to realize that there are many variables that contribute to the possibility of having deep connections. The clearest factor was my own advance mental and emotional preparations. I took time before entering into the erotic space to ground myself, so that I could connect joyfully with my queer brothers.

Yet there was another thing I observed about my high quality experiences at Eros—the visits that left me feeling holy, whole and more alive.

It seemed that on the nights when a certain attendant was at the door, the club's environment was more connective and integrated. He always greeted people warmly and he played ritualistic music (such as the music of the group Dead Can Dance). These unobtrusive touches created a feeling of entering into a sacred space, a healing temple. I spoke to him about this feeling on one

occasion. I told him that if I worked there, I would consider walking through the space with smudge, and praying before patrons arrived. It was not a surprise when he responded that he in fact did exactly that. Sacredness can be created anywhere that you go. As you learn to draw upon the essential sacredness of the world, your partner(s) and yourself, greater opportunities for
healing may become manifest.

In group work through Flesh and Spirit Community verbal contracts are made to hold the space sacred. These agreed upon guidelines are:

1. Confidentiality. Telling our stories is an important way of healing ourselves and each other. We ask that participants in a given workshop, gathering, or ritual not share another man's stories outside of this activity, with identifying information, unless you have permission.

2. Intimacy in Sacred Space. We are very intimate with each other in ritual space. A participant must not assume that intimacy translates from one exercise to the next, or outside of rit ual space. We request that all honor each other's boundaries.

This particular contract is probably one of the most essential practices in Flesh and Spirit Community. It allows men to connect, touch and experience intimacy at a level that works for them. Flesh and Spirit Community is made of men of all relationship configurations around erotic expression. This continuum contains men who only express their erotic component with the guided work we do in community together (thus who are otherwise celibate). Some men are in coupled or partnered relationships who only express their erotic selves outside their relationships when in sacred spaces like Flesh and Spirit . Yet, other men are seeking erotic connections inside and outside the community for learning, partnership, healing, pleasure, etc. Thus, this guideline allows safety for any of these men in their varied desires to come into community safely.

3. The Right to Pass. Each man has the right to choose not to participate in any exercise or ritual. Each man is invited to stretch himself, but if for some reason he needs to pass up a particlar exercise, he can inform the facilitator and step out of the process.

4. All Feelings Are Valid. All feelings are valid and appropriate. Each man is encouraged to listen to what's coming up for him without judgement of himself or others. "We all are doing the best we can."

5. Responsibility for One's Experience. "I take full responsibility for myself and thus create safety for the community." By taking care of himself, each man helps keep the group safe.

 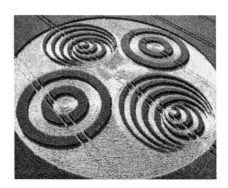

"On a recent trip to Glastonbury, England, we acquired these crop circle pictures. No matter what their origin, people told us of fascinating experiences they had while walking through these circles. The geometric shapes, whether human-made or not, solicit mysterious bodily responses."

Sacred Sites

All lands of the earth hold unique energies. The history of the land is much like that the human body. The stories making up that history are stored in the land's rocks, air/gases, water, plants, animals and structures. In addition, the human actions of war, conflict, peace, joy and reverence have a direct impact upon the land. These cumulative factors contribute to the felt experiences we have in our body in any given location.

It is my belief we are all stewards of the land. The Queer tribe may have its own unique responsibility to care for the land, assist in its healing and activate the energies the land wishes to express. My guidance spoke to me recently affirming Erotic Body Prayer is adding to the consciousness that is strengthening the spiritual immune system of the planet. As there is a stronger energetic immune system around the planet, there is more harmony and less potential for negativity such as terrorism and ecological despoilment.

Erotic Body Prayer is optimized when the hearts and bodies of those in ritual space are connected to the heart and body of the earth. My partner, Donny, and I have been privileged to create or participate in many rituals around the world. On several occasions, the rich layered red stones of Sedona, Arizona with their vortices of energy served as the location for ecstatic rituals of channeling and improvisational music. The rocks beneath our bodies seemed to stream their energy through us supporting the voice of my channeling and the sound of his violin. Recently, at the shores of the Indian Ocean on the island of Bali, Indonesia, I did some trance work, channeling on the stones of a water goddess temple . As I channeled, Donny asked my guides questions and held the space for us. The antiquity of the rocks we sat on along with the gentle waves of the sea rolling in seemed to tell their stories through the information being shared. I felt the energy expanding around my body. In the meantime, a temple beggar found his way down to where Donny and I were sitting. This man had already approached us rather aggressively when we entered the temple initially. Donny, of course, was telling him to leave. What I was able to notice even in trance was the man was changing in the energy around us and he was willing to leave rather easily. My sense was the expanded energy had pushed him away.

Subtly, but powerfully, my body experienced an example of what had been told to me earlier: just like the body of the earth, I had experienced a strengthening of my spiritual immune system , a sense of more harmony and of being less vulnerable to negativity.

Any given geographic location may be a container of great ecstasy, joy and lightness or, just as easily, of heaviness and sorrow; just as we humans are containers of "body stories" consisting of these energies, so is the earth. Most often, sites on the earth are energetically a mixture of these two polarities. Our rituals of ecstasy may play a vital part in supporting and healing ourselves and the planet. I believe cooperation from the heart and body of humans and earth will release this new evolution. Our ecstatic rituals will act like acupressure on the surface of the sacred geometry of the earth, healing, releasing, and balancing a healthy planet.

Sacred Geometry

The first international Flesh and Spirit Community retreat held in Bali, Indonesia in March, 2007 was launched in a space created out of sacred geometry. The images, symbols and structures of Sacred River Retreat Center were created from the science and intuitive information of a teacher to both Donny and myself named Shankari the Alchemist.

Shankari tells the story of designing the Sri Yantra pool at her retreat center in Bali[1] using the guidance and science of sacred geometry. Each ceramic tile was to be placed in an exact pattern to create a geometric grid. On the day the Sri Yantra pool was to be opened for a public presentation, a German scholar of Sanskrit coincidentally happened to be in residence at the retreat center. He informed Shankari that the points of the tile petals were off a few inches to be an exact replica of the symbol reported in ancient Sanskrit texts. Halting the opening of the pool, Shankari had the corrections made in construction before the pool was activated for use.

Sacred geometry assumes there are mathematical grids that formulate high vibrations for magic. The care of intention, intuitive instruction and science put into the construction of spaces such as the Sri Yantra pool in Bali, open the door for sacred work to be amplified.

Shankari also shared a story that while doing an activation ritual with a group in the Sri Yantra pool, each member of the group experienced an erotic release without physically touching each other. Sometimes just creating a sacred space for ecstatic work enables erotic energy to move through each chakra and may often be experienced as a kundalini energy rising through the body. Sacred geometry increases the potential for the highest vibrations to be expressed.

B. The Body as Sacred Temple
Our erotic spiritual journeys take us to the innermost parts of

ourselves to heal and meet with the divine. In most religious tradi-tions, temples have been the spaces where the divine has been called forth, invoked, worshiped, honored or praised. The inner-most part of the temple has often been seen as the place where the glory of God/Goddess/Spirit meets the people.

In Hinduism, one may move from the outer court of the tem-ple, passing by Ganesh (the deity of removing obstacles to enlight-enment), to the inner court, where prayers and offerings are being shared. In the innermost space (usually with a narrow entrance), the priests offer a blessing. In ancient Judaism, the temple had an outer court, an inner court called the holy place, and the inner-most court called the holy of holies. The holy of holies was where the Shekina (feminine divine name for the glory of God) would bless the offering of the priest. In Wicca, the earth is the holy place and the circle is where magic happens. Many ancient pagan reli-gions had temples where the sacred prostitutes would bless the people as they paid homage to Goddess/God. Their rituals addressed all the cycles of a person's life: birth, death, sexuality, planting and harvesting.

The temple has been seen as the container of the divine—and also as a nexus of interaction between the spiritual and physical worlds. The temple also was regarded as a unified container for all aspects of the divine. The same can be said of the human body: it is the unified and integrated temple of our spirits. As Christianity evolved, the symbolic meaning of the temple became divided over the separation of the body and spirit, but nevertheless the body was called the temple of the Holy Spirit. Claiming the body as the temple of the spirit is a key principle in Erotic Body Prayer.

The center of temple might often be correlated to the heart. The energy of unconditional love, compassion and grace. The blood feeds nutrition and life force to the whole body as the Divine spark pulsating with life.

In this text, I would highlight the thought that our genitals may actually be likened to our heart, the inner sanctum of the temple. The amount of energy that is imposed upon our genitals, hiding them, accentuating them to perform, the "no touch zone," or the keep it private/secret area means they get a great deal of energetic attention.

What we avoid or over-emphasize is always of interest to me. Integration is balance. I remember hearing Louise Hay once say, "I don't think God spends his/her time wondering about how we are using our genitals."[2]

Setting the tone for Erotic Body Prayer means seeing all parts of the body as sacred. Returning to the old religious ideas of the genitals as symbols of the sacred fertility of the earth to bring forth new life may lead us back to balance. Returning to the sacredness of the penis/lingam, the Sanskrit writings defining it as "the magic wand" or "wand of light" may bring heart back to our masculine aspect. Returning to the vagina as the Sanskrit definition of "the sacred cave," "the mysterious place of birth," may open our hearts to the secrets that have been forgotten to heal our world. In Queer people, this marriage of Shiva and Shakti (footnote to explain Shiva and Shakti) is a natural dwelling in the temple of the body.

Body as Spirit

The Body Is The Temple

Of The Holy Spirit

1 Cor 6:19[3]

In my opinion, queer people have a unique opportunity to experience the essential unity of flesh and spirit. Our bodies, the temples of our spirit, are inseparable from the divine. When we go to the innermost parts of ourselves, intentional touch becomes a powerful process of sacred connection.

Honoring our bodies as both the expression of the divine and the containers of the divine transforms how we view the body, how we experience sexuality, how we perceive spirit, and how we approach the sacred. If we can acknowledge our bodies as sacred, our gifts to each other will be changed and empowered. Overtly religious concepts, like "praising" God/Goddess/Spirit, can be frightening or distancing for many queer people, because the users of religious language have oppressed us with judgments of violence. Yet praise is a powerful tool for us to tap into spirit.

Some years ago I met one of the early long-term survivors of AIDS, Louie Nassaney. He attributed much of his ability to move through many AIDS-related conditions to his spirituality.[4] He talked about praying and praise to God as a gateway to connecting with himself. I felt a strong rapport with Louie, because we shared this practice. For me, praise has always been a gateway to greater unity of spirit. It connects me to the divine inside me, and I feel the energy spiral outward to the divine outside of me. It is in that connection that I have found a source of spiritual power. This unified, spiritual energy is always available to us; it is part of us.

Worship and the Body

If we can view our bodies as temples of praise, then we release them to become the agents of our own healing. There is a Hebrew psalm that instructs us in the proper attitude of worship as we enter into holy space. "Enter into God's gates (to the temple) with thanksgiving, and enter into God's courts with praise," says the Psalmist. For too long have we made the body a stranger to the practice of worship—leaving praise and ecstatic union with Spirit in a mental, disconnected sphere. Queer people can find a fuller experience of spiritual connection by embracing their bodies as gateways into ecstatic states of unity and praise.

Praise may be directed inward or outward, or in both directions. Entering into bodywork in a spirit of praise causes our hearts to sing, and our bodies to awaken. Both practitioners and clients will benefit by taking a moment to make a connection to a higher source of awareness, however they perceive it. Using chant, song or toning is very effective in achieving states of gratitude. Sounding can be accompanied by an intetional posture (such as hands touching the earth or hands reaching to the sky). By exercising
these simple actions, we can begin to experience the spiral dance of energy between flesh and spirit, between our own bodies and the energy surrounding us.

C. Sourcing Spirit/Energies of All That Is

The use of Archetypes may assist in this process. It is vital to use your own experience to work with spiritual energies. No religion or charismatic leader has true authority over our experience of the world around us; it's up to us to find meaning in our spiritual work. Ethereal, vague "La-la" words of the New Age, or institutional religious words may block one person from tapping the power of the universe, while they simultaneously may liberate another person. Use what works for you, and be open to reclaiming old ideas that may have been rendered against you in the past. As queer people, we can choose to reclaim whatever is good in traditional philosophy and religion for our own purposes.

Sourcing spirit means welcoming energies that are loving and kind to be present. What does that mean for you? Sometimes spiritual guides or sensations seem more like psychological notions than actual sources of energy. Play with sources in your spiritual practice and notice how you feel. Allow your imagination to be a tool of discovery.

In my own Erotic Body Prayer practice, I utilize many different systems for invoking spirit. As a Reiki master, I simply access symbols and words to open myself to energy or life force. I also welcome the spirits of masters, healers, and others who have touched my life. Likewise, the energies of nature—Earth and Sky—are extremely vibrant sources of connection for me.

Animals and plants often speak to our souls, and their energies support us. Sometimes we meet animal "guides" in our dreams; always pay attention to dreams that involve animals, because they could be bringing you very powerful messages. For example, a snake came to me in a dream once and said, "You are on the path of the snake." Since I had this dream, I often welcome the spirit of the snake in doing my work.

Openness to spirit can help us make pivotal life decisions. When I first considered starting my work, which I called "Flesh and Spirit," I experienced several confirming events that shaped

my strategy. I often chant or pray when I am driving in my car; it can be calming and centering, and help me resolve ideas or emotional issues. Once while I was chanting in my car, I literally felt the presence of someone with me. I recognized the presence as my dear friend Ted, whom I had worked with in the Healing Circle of Cincinnati. In my mind and body, the following words formed: "Kirk, I want to help you with the erotic spiritual work you are planning." It was an unmistakable message of support, and it helped me move forward with great faith in this major
career change.

Being a psychotherapist at the time, I was well aware that some of my colleagues might have a difficult time accepting the legitimacy of this experience. Therefore I went to see a friend, Victor, who is a psychic by profession. I wanted to see if he could shed some light on my experience. I told Victor I felt someone's presence come to me. With just that one piece of information, Victor said, "I sense someone name Theodore around you, and he wants to help you with some new work you are creating." Victor did not know anything about my new work, nor did he know Ted; it was a remarkable confirmation of my own spiritual experience.

The ability to connect with spirit will often grow, expand and change as you develop a healing journey, and become more whole. No matter how you understand "sourcing" spirit, it is a starting place to move into the sacred world, particularly in bodywork. My experience of Ted coming to me could have been a part of my own consciousness speaking—certainly that is how many people would interpret that experience. But the confirmation of spirit and the sense of connection radically changed the way I practice healing work. In this respect, sourcing spirit really can change what happens in our lives and in our work.

D. Energy Education and Work

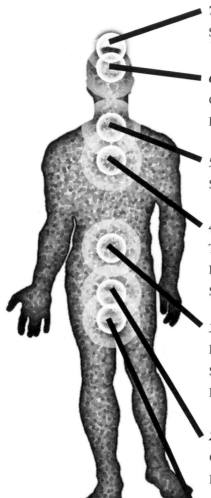

7th - *Connection to God/Goddess/All that is*
Sourcing love and wisdom

6th - *Intuition/Spiritual Nature*
Gathering information for touch and healing
Discerning the truth

5th - *Expression/Communication*
Speaking your truth through love

4th - *Compassion/Love*
Transforming our fear through love
Letting go of Judgement
Staying free of attachment to outcome

3rd - *Personal Power*
Being our own authority
Setting and expanding boundaries
Facing/resolving conflict

2nd - *Sexuality/Creativity*
Charging the body and soul
Live life passionately

1st - *Physical Survival*
Uses Instincts to bring life and love

There is growing interest among scientists in the study of energy medicine, as well as the ancient traditions that teach healing through energy work. Healers use traditions that name the energy as chi, ki, chakras, Shakti, prana, deeksha, auras, "Rivers of Living Water," Holy Spirit, and life force. Although these frameworks can be immensely helpful to us, the greatest wisdom comes through your own experience of listening through the body. Listen acutely to the sensations of your body to find the clues or markers of the energy flows in your body.

Among the various conceptual frameworks that describe energy flows, the system of chakras is the most useful in my own experience. The chakra system describes how one holds, gathers, discharges and exchanges energy. The chakra system identifies seven major energy centers that follow the direction of the spinal cord. These energy centers radiate outward from the body, and with skill, may be sensed by others. Each center has an aspect, function or purpose that it weaves into the whole energy aura. The illustration indicates the place and function of each chakra. These energies interact with everything we touch as we move through the environment.

This energy field emanating out from the body is the interactive force of life given and received by each person. This field exchanges messages for wholeness, healing, protection and woundedness.

When my chakras interact with your chakras, the potentials and possibilities are profound. The following section speaks to healing. However, the interaction of one's energetic field may lend itself to conflict or harmonizing conflict as well. The principles of the new warrior originating from Morihei Ueshiba says, "Your spirit is the true shield. Opponents confront us continually, but actually there is no opponent there. Enter deeply into an attack and neutralize it as you draw that misdirected force into your own sphere."[5]

A year long training class for healers in Flesh and Spirit is called Energy Medicine. Many men of Flesh and Spirit have gone through this class becoming Reiki masters in the concluding class. For our retreat, "the Ecstatic Path," every man in Flesh and Spirit received the Level I attunement to Reiki. It seems the developing power of Flesh and Spirit is related to its approach to the ecstatic and erotic work from an energetic/spiritual perspective.

I would like to introduce each man of Flesh and Spirit Community to the basics of Reiki to keep the unity, power and reverence of this simple system held in the community. Here is some basic information about Reiki and its origins. Creating communities with an energetic foundation, such as Reiki, enhances the ease of doing ecstatic work.

A Parable of Usui

A Japanese mystic, Dr. Usui, sought the wisdom and power of healing which he saw lacking in Japan during the early 20th century. On his quest, her studied the texts and writings of ancient Buddhism. It is said Usui found an abbot who encouraged him to take the formula he had gathered from the ancient writings to Mt. Koriyama, to fast and pray. The formula seemed to indicate doing a ritual for twenty-one days.

Usui encircled himself in twenty one stones for each day. Each day he would throw away a stone waiting for the revelation of healing to be imparted. On the darkest part of the night before the dawn, he threw out the last stone and nothing had happened.

Usui had been told that the light of healing might possibly kill him if it struck him. In that moment, he saw the light appear. He had to choose whether he wanted to receive the light with its potential for healing or overpowering him. The story goes that Usui, hit by the light, receiving the revelation of each symbol he had studied with its meaning and usage.

This story of Usui seems to describe the ecstatic path as many of us are seekers of healing, willing to risk our lives to find the revelation of love made manifest. Reiki offers a simple model and process to enhance the power of healing intrinsic in all of us and increase our psychic abilities for the highest good of all.

The three basic symbols Usui supposedly saw in this mystical experience were as follows:

Cho Ko Rei

This is a symbol that charges a space for healing to be activated. It is also a symbol for opening the Reiki practitioner to increased healing power for physical healing.

Sei He Kei

This is a symbol of emotional and mental healing. This symbol is especially supportive for those wishing to change cognitive behavioral patterns or addictive processes.

Hon Sha Ze Sho Nen

This is a symbol used when the practitioner is unable to physically touch the body of the receiver. This symbol transcends time and space making accessible healing energy to anyone, anywhere.

Using Reiki in combination with erotic work may broaden the potentials for wholeness to be experienced. In Flesh and Sprit, we developed a process of two practitioners offering Reiki to brothers on a massage table. One practitioner would use the traditional sequences of still touch hand patterns on the upper body, channeling Reiki, while the other practitioner strokes the lower body, including the genitals. Each

practitioner is a Reiki channel, one actively pleasuring, and the other with no movement in the exchange. We call this ecstatic Reiki weaving hot and cool energies together.

Another version of ecstatic Reiki was developed for our Ecstatic Path Retreat. We designed four roles to be shared, in a ritual inspired by the archetype of the Sacred Prostitute as erotic healer. Each man was attuned to Reiki Level I before doing this ritual.# With the recipient of healing lying on a massage table, the Sacred Prostitute, the principal practitioner, offered the receiver touch, massage, and erotic connection (if desired). The other two men served as Reiki "current workers,"* and sat around the massage table, touching neither the recipient nor the practitioner.

*Current workers is a term used by the famous Brazilian healer , John of God. John of God had group of people play, meditate or direct energy to him while he does his healing work. These people are called current workers. Donny and I got to do some work with John of God and be current workers for hours at a time. This was very powerful work

These current workers used the distant healing technique of Reiki to focus on the Sacred Prostitute as he offered healing. The interaction of all these roles with thirty men wove an unforgettable ecstatic community experience.

Body Scanning

As I introduce queer men to Erotic Body Prayer, I take time to gain a sense of the energy outside the body. Some energy workers refer to this as "aura reading". I call the technique body scanning. I move my hands a few inches over the body without touching the client's skin. This is a very effective way to begin sensing the variations of individual energy patterns. Slow movements over each chakra can provide the bodyworker with a wealth of information as he/she listens to the subtleties of sensations. It is common to experience sensations like warmth, heat, coolness, density, thinness, softness, tingling, pulsation and vibration.

If we can open our minds to the belief that we are "more than just bodies", we can touch in a way that is loving, powerful and healing no matter what our erotic or physical desires may be. Body scanning is a very effective means of identifying not only what energies are at play within the client's body, but also how one's own energies interact with the client's. Therefore it is a very grounding practice for sacred intimates to use, and it can help guide both practitioner and client to the highest good and most
healing type of erotic touch to use in a session.

Directing Energy

Another, more playful tool to share energy without physical touch is directing energy with thought. This is another simple but powerful process. It involves verbal interaction as well as nonverbal interaction. Tell your partner what part of his body you are direct-

ing energy to, hold that thought or intention, and notice what both of you feel. Practice that for a while, and then try it without sharing where you are focusing
your attention. What happens?

I offer an occasional, short workshop called "Nipple Play: Charging the Body & Soul".

In conducting an intake interview for the workshop, I use the process of directing energy. In one intake interview, my partner directed energy to me, focusing on my heart. He did not say where he was focusing the energy. Nonetheless, I immediately felt a warm sensation across my heart and chest, running down to my cock and back up to my eyes.

All around my eyes I could feel warmth, and relaxation of my eye muscles. This was a significant and very wonderful experience for me, because my vision is often challenged due to cataracts, causing me fatigue around my eyes. This simple connection of energy brought a great ease to my vision. As we moved into using touch and nipple play to increase the connection, this sense of relief in my eyes only increased.

As with most techniques and practices, there is usually a counter principle. While one may direct energy with thought/intention or direct energy by the physical placement of hands (or other body parts), the counter principle is that energy goes where it is needed. In Reiki, there are specific hand placements to begin to focus the energy however ultimately the energy does what the "intelligence" directs regardless of the focus of the hand placements.

Using the Reiki mantra Hon Sha Ze Sho Nen seems to magnify the benefits to the person who is receiving (that is not present).

Reed Waller, a leader in Flesh and spirit, has facilitated numerous Ecstatic Massage Rituals and Self-Pleasuring Rituals as a means of Erotic Body Prayer. These sessions are framed as "puja," from the Hindu concept of an offering to a deity. In Erotic Body Prayer, sacred pleasure is the offering to the Divine, a directing of the energy outward as Hon Sha Ze Sho Nen to the Source itself. This outer directedness allows the pleasure to be the vehicle of changing consciousness beyond that of the people performing the erotic puja.

E. Boundary Setting:
- **Saying yes, saying no**
- **Connection and separation**
- **Boundaries that fit**

The art of living with clarity is not taught formally in schools and colleges, but it may be learned through mentoring and living consciously. Unfortunately, in our busy lives, most of us spend a lot of time giving and receiving mixed messages. Ultimately, if we wish to experience more clarity in our lives, we need to learn to become clearer ourselves.

Therefore listening to the "Yes" and "No" messages of our body is a very useful practice.

Sometimes the mind cannot deliver a clear answer, because the issue is just too complex, there are too many conflicting consequences, and so on. Our bodies provide simpler messages that can liberate us from our conundrums. Most effective leaders throughout the ages have been able to trust their body wisdom and make momentous decisions based on what their full range of experience tells them. In day to day living, being able to say "Yes" or "No" fully is a key to right actions. The skill of living in your "Yes" or "No" is a crucial foundation for boundary setting in all situations.

As spoken of earlier, I offer a one-day, experiential workshop called *The Peaceful Warrior*. In this workshop we use an Aikido exercise that invites the body to experience the physical energies of "Yes" and "No." These movements help us recognize what it feels like to choose either "Yes" or "No" in our bodies. The goal of the exercise is to learn how to operate with an open, neutral and loving attitude as we make decisions.

In Erotic Body Prayer, telling the truth that comes up is the foundation for learning how to say "Yes" and "No". As we heal, letting go of guilt, shame and judgments held in the body, we learn to create boundaries that reflect our wholeness and congruence. The experience of breaking through to clarity is enormously liberating.

For example, I worked with a client over time whose erotic energy would shift in dramatic ways. While working with Bruno, his excitement and hunger for erotic touch would grow, and yet there would be moments when he would simply "check out" and would feel like he was ten feet away from me. I persisted in asking him what he was experiencing. He said, "Well, I feel ashamed. I love this, but I'm not sure my lover would be okay with me doing this." His mixed "Yes" and "No" took us to his shame and guilt, freeing us both to discover how to proceed in a caring and holistic manner. We were able to transform the session to bring healing and freedom within agreements that felt honest.

An Aikido exercise used to experience "no" energetically and as neutral.

Boundaries That Fit

For Erotic Body Prayer to be effective, both practitioner and client must be able to build effective boundaries before the work begins. Because the practitioner is a sexual healer, a bodyworker, and a spiritual counselor, there is an added duty on him or her to be proactive and willing to work with integrity.

In my practice of integrative bodywork, I have implemented a number of steps that are necessary before I will offer an Erotic Body Prayer session. First and foremost, I must have some degree of spiritual connection with the client. The most effective way to develop this is to offer a traditional massage first, weaving some erotic touch into the experience, if the client desires it. In this initial session, I become aware of the client's energy flow, wounds, and personal intentions to grow or heal. I ask the client whether he would prefer me to wear clothing or be unclothed. I explain that erotic touch simply means massaging the whole body, including the genitals.

In the initial session I start with energy work. Next, I offer head and neck massage. The client will then turn over (face down) on the table. At all times, I assess the comfort and connection of both of us, since the energy moves in both directions. If the client has said he wants some erotic touch, I would lean down, and we will embrace. This enables us to have a moment to connect more deeply. I find that this embrace reveals a great deal of information about the client's comfort, hunger, boundaries, etc. I continue to listen to the client's responses, including breath, vocalization, mutual touching and muscle tissue reactions. This reveals further information about how the energy and process of connection is proceeding. With this information, I continue to set boundaries that feel loving and respectful for both of us.

Intake Interview

All the work of Flesh and Spirit Community involves the broad understanding of Erotic Body Prayer. Thus, prior to doing a workshop with Flesh and Spirit Community, an intake interview prepares interested men for the work. This interview allows the gleaning of information about the man's boundaries through questions from the Peaceful Warrior workshop.

Here are three segments of that interview process:

Part 1

The general questions include:

1. Who is in your support system? (Especially, who can you share anything with?).
2. How do you take care of your body?
3. What do you "know" spiritually. What do you hold true?
4. What is drawing you to join Flesh & Spirit Community / to do this work?

Part 2

The second section of questions looks at "body stories" as they pertain to themes of the peaceful warrior work:

- Asking for help
- Living in your "yes" and living in your "no"
- Setting boundaries and exploring new boundaries

- Dealing with conflict heartfully
- Being your own authority

1. Thinking about your family of care growing up, what did you see as far as asking for help? Did you have models for asking for help?

Pertaining to the three inner positions of needy, powerful and centered, these questions are asked:

2. When you walk through the Castro, or anywhere in San Francisco, you will almost stumble over homeless people. What do you experience in your body when you see homeless people (especially in the first few seconds)?

3. What do you feel in your body when you are powerful?

4. What do you feel in your body when you are centered?

5. When every part of you is in "yes" (body, words, actions and energy) what do you feel in your body?

"When every part of you experienced "no," what do you feel in your body?

6. When you feel fear, what does fear feel like in your body?

7. What does compassion feel like in your body?

8. When you are approaching conflict, what do you feel in your body?

9. In conclusion, if you could transform the fears on your life, what would you be like? (your body, relationships, work and play)

Part 3

The last section is a body experience.

The purpose of this part is to notice the subtlety of "body stories" felt energetically without physical touch, with light touch and with sensual / erotic touch. These exercises are not meant to take the interviewee into any specific place or state, but to notice the stories that arise through sensation and feelings through the body.

Doorways

The intake interview for the peaceful warrior is also used for the energy medicine class and the ecstatic gatekeepers retreat. These are the doorways into the community and work of Flesh & Spirit.

This experiential interview process is done with the client's eyes closed. I conduct a series of quick exercises to assess the client's responses. Each exercise helps me listen to the sensations in the client's body. Having the client recognize personal space, and the power of "Yes" and "No" are important goals for the interview.

Conducting interviews like this carries benefit not only for the client, but for me as well. The process opens up my compassion, and helps me discover whether I can connect easily with the client, or whether I feel disconnected. With the collective information from the verbal questions and experiential exercises, I can assess

how ready the client is to do this kind of work, and what my own boundaries might be.

Men who regard their sexuality as sacred can find many ways to explore these questions, which relate to their own ability to give and receive love. For this reason, these practices have great value, no matter what the setting. For me, the most essential step is to challenge myself to move beyond shape and form, regarding each man I connect with as a sacred and whole person. It is also vital to being congruent and true to myself. I believe our work is to offer our gifts to each other with as much congruence of body, mind, spirit/heart as possible. If we can undertake this effort using the fullness of our erotic bodies, we may find that our lives can be filled with greater freedom, joy and release from the wounds of the past.

As with all new experiences, the willingness to allow mistakes is very important. Grace yourself with permission to make mistakes as you learn more about connections, boundaries and intentions. Indeed, "grace" means gift, so give yourself the gift of what the zen masters call "Beginner's Mind". You are not always going to feel connected in all the ways you could hope for; let that be part of the learning.

(A video of this process can be found on the internet at http://www.fleshandspirit.org/iiframe.html.)

"Keep love in your heart. A life without it

is like a sunless garden

when the flowers are dead. The conscious-

ness of loving and being loved brings a

warmth and richness to life that nothing

else can bring."

Oscar Wilde (1854–1961)

F. Pathways to Prayer through the Body

Still Touch

As the Erotic Body Prayer session unfolds, intentional touch is lovingly introduced. The process of sensing energy without physical touch begins the information exchange that deepens as still touch, or the laying on of hands, is introduced. Laying one's hands on the client's body begins a tactile, vibrant conversation between two partners.

If you have learned to be clear about what you are feeling in your body before you touch someone else, you have a baseline knowledge of your own experience, which helps in separating your own reactions from the client's reactions. As you place your hand on another person's body, you may experience a new sensation in your body. This is one of the fascinating truths of bodywork: we can exchange actual, tactile experience directly. The sensations you feel in your own body may originate with the other person.

Skillful practitioners learn how to differentiate between these experiences. This can help in guiding the client directly to the places of healing that are available to him.

I have long noticed that when I touch someone, especially when I'm focused and attentive, I experience what is happening in my client's body as though it were happening in my own body. For example, I may notice a tight feeling over my forehead, as I work on a client. If so, I ask the client whether he is experiencing sinus problems, headaches, or some discomfort over his forehead. Also if the symptom is not physical, I will ask about mental overload. This exchange of verbal information supports the body the processes that are already underway.

It is crucial to directly communicate with the client as you experience exchanges of energy. Gathering information and assigning an interpretation without having confirmation from the other person can be dangerous—misleading the practitioner or setting up an inequality in power. If the practitioner can take the time to check out his experience, then practitioner and client can become teachers and students to each other.

Shamans and healers use their special awareness of energy forces to gather this kind of information. At first, the experience may feel like a "disease" symptom in your body. Thus, it is important to see yourself as a channel of healing energy that offers help to clear whatever the other person is releasing. Practitioners are well-served by regarding themselves as channels of energy, instead of "vessels" for other people's infirmities; this enables them to free themselves quickly from unwanted symptoms.

These exchanges of information are constantly occurring, but most of us have not paid much attention. Some people have a partial awareness of how they communicate energetically, they but lack a language that adequately describes what they are feeling.

Because the exchange of energy involves physical touch, it is intimate and powerful. It is important for practitioners to stay ware of this communication, because intimacy and power roles can distract us from the healing aspects of our work, leading us into unproductive projections. For true healing to occur we need to stay free of judgment, both of ourselves and of others. For this very reason, touch at the beginning of an Erotic Body Prayer session accelerates the process of mutual trust.

As mutual trust builds, very specific healing can happen. For example, one client, Jim, seemed to have trouble with his hearing. I placed my hands on his belly and I noticed a congested pressure in my left ear. So I asked Jim, "Is something going on in your left ear?" "Yes," he said, "I'm just getting over an ear infection." That became a starting place for using the information we were sharing through our bodies for greater delight and adventure, using very still and simple methods of touch.

Clearing Exercise

Since Erotic Body Prayer is such an intimate healing process, staying clear energetically is crucial. One does pick up the energies of another person, thus having techniques to stay free will allow one to keep on vibrantly as a healer. If attention is not paid to clearing you will become, as one of my colleagues says, "another healer down while healing."

In the midst of a session, you may not have time to do a full clearing process, but a simple intention of clearing will dissipate much. Affirming any energy that does not serve you and your client's highest good be gone, into the earth into the light (or where you send things" will have immediate benefit.

Often after a session I may do a more extensive ritual of smudging of a visualization/mediation I call the violet flame.

The Violet Flame Ritual

The violet flame or purple flame can be found in a variety of spiritual traditions. It has been reclaimed in the early 1900's by Elizabeth and Mark Prophet as a tool for karmic clearing.[6] Versions of this simple ritual are appearing among numerous spiritual healing communities in this new age environment of ecumenism.

This version is a synthesis of my guidance to use for the Teaching Reiki Master Class.

A welcoming of the white or golden light into the space as an invocation is called upon:

Come!

A release of any energy that is not of love and light is commanded to leave the space.

Go! (Followed by three claps.)

A visualization will follow, seeing yourself surrounded by the white or golden light. Guardians (ancestors, holy ones, angels etc.) are welcome to stand in protection as you stand in this white light. They will hold this space with you.

Then, imagine the area around your body containing / expressing your energy field.

Begin to see a violet flame burning away all the old stories (body stories, psychological stories, spiritual stories, or karmic stories) that are being held in your energy field. Let the violet flame be a freeing agent to your attachments that do not offer wholeness. You may imagine this burning away or clearing for this life time or past life times.

After using the violet flame to clear, seal the space around your energy field with the white or golden light.

Complete the ritual by breathing the energy up and down your chakras from the earth to sky, sky to earth.

Finish with three claps.

Caressing

There are many subtle ways in which touch can offer important information, without ever awakening pleasure in the body. However, when simple movements or stroking over an area of the body are added to the session, invoking subtle experiences of pleasure becomes an additional aspect to promoting healing. In numerous workshops I have led men through simple exercises where they stroked each other's faces. Their reactions to this simple process have ranged from feelings of comfort, soothing, arousal, vulnerability and longing, to fear anger and discomfort. Because these experiences were intentional and safe, they allowed men to open up even more, and to learn how their bodies were speaking to them. It is so rare that we truly stop to take the time to listen to our bodies; when we do so, we can quickly enter into the delight of healing work. These responses are body stories making themselves known through sensations and feelings in the body.

Firm Touch and Deep Healing

Firm touch, or deep tissue work, is another means of bringing blood, oxygen and energy to the areas to be touched. Because firm touch involves substantial energy, it will often solicit varied responses to strength and power. These can range from ecstasy to the sudden emergence of a traumatic memory, so it is very important to gain a good awareness of the client's overall emotional state before invoking firm touch.

Sometimes deeper wounds will become more evident. For example, the craving to be "being taken care of" manifests very often. Wounding from unequal relationships (emotional, physical and energetic) is another issue that emerges through the body as firm touch is applied, but when the practitioner combines firm touch with the clearly stated understanding of safety, the client can begin to transform old wounds held in body memory. Because firm touch calls for even more attentiveness, it is very helpful to ask the question, "What do you wish to heal?" as firm touch is applied.

I have a deep respect for the power of firm touch to heal. I am sexual abuse survivor myself, and over the course of my own life, I have found that receiving firm touch (deep tissue), safely applied by trustworthy men, has been one of the most significant processes I have experienced.

Deep tissue work on my muscular tissue has opened up feelings of fear, panic and vulnerability that I did not know I possessed. Once I became more aware of how my body stored the grief and pain associated with trauma, I became more skillful in healing my own history of abuse. My body was my most important teacher in this process; by trusting the messages it was sending me, I entered into a larger, more spacious world. I learned a greater capacity to love and forgive, and to reach out to others in support of their healing process. I do not believe that I would have experienced such transformational self-love without the discovery of energy flow within my body, and the ways in which we can facilitate its flow.

Anal Massage

There is another aspect to my own healing journey as a sexual abuse survivor. Because I experienced sustained sexual abuse over many months, I have had many unpleasant, even painful memories. These memories troubled me particularly whenever I attempted to explore the erotic dimensions of my ass. For many years of my adult life, I felt "shut down" in this area—which, given my history, was a reasonable response to trauma.

In the context of sacred space with a group of brothers, I explored an ecstatic anal massage as a way to heal these painful memories. I explained to my fellow queer brothers that I was a sexual abuse survivor and I needed them to be sensitive to my requests if I asked them to stop the

massage. I also asked them to be especially sensitive to my non-verbal cues, particularly if I looked like I suddenly "checked out" from the process. In the safety of our contracts and intention for healing, I had an ecstatic experience of pleasure that was liberating and empowering. Another thread of my (sexual abuse) body story was complete, freeing all my body up for ecstasy.

Genital Play

I do not wish to duplicate techniques that have been widely disseminated by the erotic spiritual pioneer, Joseph Kramer. His work introduced Queer men to creating safety and permission to heartfully touch lingam together. His educational materials are valuable for developing techniques for genital stimulation.[7]Essential themes to genital pleasuring as a conductor of energy would be: create a system with the client for feedback, slow down and focus on your client's pleasure while staying in your joyfulness. Gather feedback about how to touch (light, firm, sensitivities) before beginning the process. Minimize words in your system of feedback. Words take you to old stories. Allow the pleasure to create a new experience with yourself. Moans and groans are

great because they vibrate the system releasing old stories and awakening new ones. If words are useful, keep it simple such as red, yellow, green or yes, more, slow, or pause.

Slow down, pleasure is worth savoring. It allows healing energy to replace whatever the existing story is. Unless it has been specifically contracted, ejaculation is not the intention. And even if ejaculation has been agreed upon as possible, pleasure is the vehicle for healing. Think of all the time you have spent experiencing painful or challenging events. Slow down and allow pleasure to rewrite some of those stories.

Speed of strokes and locations and amounts of pressure are important variables to communicate about. The corona of the cock, the shaft, the balls, the scrotum, and the perineum are all valid areas to provide pleasure. With FTM brothers, the speed and pressure of strokes are particularly important. Pleasure has nothing to do with enduring something. Be clear and stay clear. For men (or women) who may have premature ejaculation or climax, using breathwork in combination with other techniques will lend itself to a sense of mastery of one's body. Also, the use of a squeeze technique at the base of the shaft of the penis will constrict the blood flow interrupting or slowing down unwanted ejaculation.

Finally, enjoy touching another's genitals. Undo the cultural stories and heal yourself every time you deliciously stroke a cock or genital area. It is your joy and the joy of the client that brings a new consciousness. Drop the fear you have of bodies and especially genitals and your heart will open. Give yourself permission to touch consciously.

G. Ecstatic Tools and Techniques

In Erotic Body Prayer, we can approach deeply felt wounds like abuse with great love and mindfulness. Introducing erotic pleasure into a session awakens the energy more powerfully, and the practitioner must be attentive to the healing intentions of the client.

There are many techniques that can assist the process. These include polarity, posturing, breath and sensory work (sound/toning, smell, temperature, sight and lubrication).

Polarity / Posturing / Yoga

Instinctively, we all know about energy flows in our lovemaking and erotic connections. This is popularly referred to as "Chemistry" between two people. However, when we embark on a conscious journey of raising energy, we can enter into entirely new realms of pleasure and ecstasy.

The chakra system provides an excellent framework for understanding the flow of energy in the body. In Tantric practices, a key objective is to build the "charge" of energy within the body, and channel it up the spinal column, touching all chakras in succession.

As energy rises from the base chakra, which is centered on the perineum, to the crown chakra (at the top of the head) erotic delight and healing can be greatly magnified.

As queer men, many of our love making positions naturally encourage that kind of energy flow. For example, one wonderful position for physical contact is the combination of genital-to-ass, or genital-to-genital touch, together with the placement of the hands on the chest, nipples or head. Positions like this, used in conjunction with breath, verbalized intentions or sound/toning can produce amazing flows of energy. Moreover, practicing positions like this can reinforce the fundamental joy of giving and

receiving, which can occur outside the dynamics of topping/bottoming, particularly as expressed in equal power relationships. Erotic Body Prayer can provide healing to those of us that have long inhabited the super-charged sexual environment of the queer men's community, helping us reclaim the fun and joy of unconditional love in our sex play. If the shared goal is healing and only healing, then we free our minds and body to experience

new levels of joy and awareness.

Ecstatic work is a way of reprogramming the old stories into new ones. How the body is postured clearly impacts the flow of energy or kundalini up the spine. Some forms of yoga have been developed with the intention to investigate the body's consciousness and open it up. B.K.S. Iyengar's work in yoga speaks directly to what I call body stories.

Incorporating yoga into ecstatic body work allows the consciousness of the body to become an Erotic Body Prayer.

Breath

We can move energy through thought, both spoken and unspoken. We can also utilize movement, posturing and forms of touch (still, caressing, firm and erotic). We can move energy through sensory work using the vibration sound (from, or to one's body). Smells from the body, aromas, and temperatures both warm and cool, the visual sight of that which is pleasing, and lubricants that ease friction all contribute to a sacred experience.

Yet the most significant facilitator of healing work is the energy of breath.

The Greek word for breath is "pneuma". It also can be interpreted to mean "spirit". This is not a coincidence. Breath awakens the body spirit/energy connection like no other tool. However, breath also requires discipline. Because serious breath work requires commitment and considerable labor, it can seem unappealing to many. It also has unpredictable outcomes in how the body may open up and emote. It is just as likely for painful wounds to awaken as it is to experience pure ecstasy. For this reason, breath work requires letting go of control. When the body is well oxygenated, sensation is heightened, body memory enlivened, and altered states will occur. It is essential to fully give oneself over to the experience, and let it be whatever it may be.

There are many breath techniques, each of which has multiple benefits. Queer men who begin to explore breath work will find that some of these breath techniques are especially effective and that others are less effective. Part of the adventure of breath work is to try different strategies that produce the states desired.

Whole Belly Breathing

Many rebirthers, holotropic breath workers, prana yama yoga instructors and sexual healers commonly use whole belly breathing as a technique to raise the energy from the lowest chakras to the highest chakras, creating a cycle of energy. To try whole belly breathing, hold your hand over your belly and take in a large full breath, extending the belly out. Use the mouth both to inhale and exhale fully. Then try inhaling through the nose and exhaling out through the mouth. Use each technique to see which produces what results for you.

Anal Breathing

Anal breathing involves moving energy downward, through the abdomen and directly out the asshole. As you inhale, relax your outer sphincter and pelvic floor (pubococcygeal or PC muscle). On the exhalation, allow the pelvic floor to relax even further, letting your energy and attention sink further down. Some teachers of anal breathing also lead the client in visualizations during the breath work, inviting the client to see his asshole relaxing as breath moves through it. As a variation, and to practice increasing your awareness and your ability to let go, try clenching and releasing the PC muscle (this is called a Kegel exercise), and clench and release the sphincter. The latter is called, in tantra, a "root lock" or *mulabandha*. Most anal breathing is very relaxing and centering, but the root lock can unleash some powerful energy. Try different techniques that match visualization with body movement and breath , and notice how you track your energy flows.

Quick Inhalation

Quickly inhale and exhale through the nose to try another common breath. This often is thought of as a detoxification breath or clearing breath. It also raises energy quickly, and is an excellent means of deepening a breath work session.

Spinal Column Breathing

At the International Somatics Conference 1996, Continuum Movement founder Emilie Conrad spoke of a breath she teaches for healing because of the vibrations it sends down the spinal column. She uses this breath with patients with spinal cord injuries to bring motion to areas of the body where nerve-activated movement cannot occur. This breath technique requires curling the tongue backwards, and touching the roof of the mouth while breathing in and out, opening up the throat and trying to breath at random intervals rather than with regularity. The breath can create a serpentine undulation of the body.

As a Reiki master, I have used a breath very similar to this in doing initiations into Reiki mastery. This kind of breath seems very ancient as a tool for spiritual work. It may have been used in Egypt or even by the healing Buddhas. Regardless of its history, it has a unique quality to it. I also use this technique in one of my workshops, which is called "The Sacred Prostitute: Midwifing the Dying". This breath sounds like and looks like "the death rattle" breath that appears in the dying. Using this breath may open up a sense of remembering on a very cellular level.

Pacing Breath

All of these breath techniques can be used at fast or slow paces. Finding some regularity to the pace is helpful. Erratic shifts may cause unusual sensations called "tetne", in which the hands or fingers may curl and hold rigid involuntarily. This is a normal phenomenon and will pass as a more regulated pace is achieved. Moving other parts of the body canalso be helpful

All traditions that speak of moving energy, or "uncoiling the kundalini", use breath work as a basic tool. In Erotic Body Prayer, you may experiment with each kind of breathing as you begin to name your intention for healing.

Big Draw: Bridge Between The Worlds

The Big Draw, a Taoist energy technique promulgated by Taoist teacher Mantak Chia, has opened many doors for Queer men to explore ecstatic energy. Joseph Kramer pioneered the use of the Big Draw in an erotic healing context by incorporating it into his Taoist/Tantric Erotic Massage Ritual. This ritual synthesizes elements of erotic massage, tantra, rebirthing breathwork, and Taoist energy healing. The Big Draw, probably ancient in practice, consists of an isometric exercise, clenching all the muscles in the body (including  the root lock) while holding one's breath, followed by a complete release and normal breathing. Breath coaches and pranayama practitioners speak of many awakenings in the body through the breath techniques mentioned above. The addition of the Big Draw, which I like to call "the bridge between the worlds" has powerful implications. Practitioners often precede the Big Draw with holotropic breath, extended full-belly breathing or quick inhalations, and the body is activated by an infusion of oxygen and prana (or chi). When this technique is used, a kundalini wave of energy uncoils promoting altered and ecstatic states that can range from grief to joy to serene relaxation and acceptance. For me this experience is consistently one that bridges the worlds and taps into a mystic realm.

Light, Color, and Nutrition

Vibrational medicine is another emerging term that describes the movement of energy by and through the body from external and internal sources. This next set of ecstatic tools lend themselves to shifting vibrations that support altered states for healing. In this section,I wish to acknowledge briefly three common factors that contribute to these vibrational states: light, color and nutrition.

Light, the metaphor of spiritual evolution, is essential to create health in the ecstatic aspirant. It is well known that persons living in areas of the world with diminished light may experience more depression.Thus, light treatments are often used in alleviating seasonal affective disorders. Color in one's surroundings (nature, walls, clothing, minerals or lighting) may contribution of a sense of well-being.

Queer folk stereotypically seen as artists and healers are often manipulating light and color to change the environment. The ambiance of a dimmer switch, candles and color seem almost required by some. Whether or not Queer folk have a special relationship with them or not, the light and color set the tone for enhancing mood, emotion and ecstasy.

At a Sacred Prostitute Retreat held by Flesh & Spirit brothers the color red was introduced to all the rituals and ceremonies. Eggs whose yolks and whites had been carefully blown out were painted red for the rituals. Red shawls were worn each session. To offset the red, only white candles and flowers adorned the space. Ritual, chant, erotic touch charged the atmosphere which had been enhanced by color and light.

Nutrition is being added to this list as a notation. The building blocks of nutrient fuel support or hinder the sustainability of an ecstatic life. Conscious fasting used for cleansing and altered states may be beneficial at times. However, nutrient absorption and transmission seem essential for optimum well-being. There are many nutritional practitioners out there as resources to investigate, so I would only add a body awareness into your discernment process for yourself. My guides have often encouraged those I'm working with to have a relationship with their food. When you go to the grocery pick up the food and notice what you feel in your body. Similarly, you might use muscle testing as a way of clarifying which food/nutrient might be helpful to you now. Finally, offering a blessing to that which you take into your body creates a better message system for your body to welcome its absorption for wholeness.

Sound/Toning

Toning, or the use of vocalized sound over parts of the body, can quickly shift energy and bring a feeling of playfulness. Toning has been used by many cultures as a healing technique. When used in Erotic Body Prayer, it opens up the body more fully. It

is especially effective to apply toning to the chakra centers, particularly the hara and the heart and root chakras. In the work of Flesh and Sprit Community called "The Sacred Prostitute" I created the use of toning as depicted above. Using plastic wrap to sanitize the process, a sheet of wrap is placed over the anus so the practitioner can tone directly up the spinal column. Using a variety of tones seems to vibrate up the spine through each chakra. Experiment with tones and different vocal sounds to see where the vibration is felt in the recipient's body and what emotions and sensations are that emerge with each tone. A simple "om" and "ah" are good starting places. It is said each chakra has its own tone. The tones of the musical scale (do, re, mi, fa, etc) are thought of as the steps through each chakra starting with "do," the first chakra. Using the techniques of Reiki, the practitioner might hold intention for the mouth (rather than the hands) to be the channel through which the life force energy flows. Using the first two mantras for physical and emotional healing might be another way of "amping up" the charge. Try using "cho" toned, "ku"(or "ko") toned, then "rei" toned, activating the power for healing to begin, followed by "sei" toned, "he" toned and "kei" toned to activate emotional healing. This intimate process can be a powerful clearing and balancing technique in ecstatic work.

There are growing bodies of research on sound and music used for healing. Research is underway investigating sounds and tones that create environments for healing or even eradicate cancer cells.[8] Anecdotally, music and sound are used to relax, excite and move people into ecstatic states. Sounds, like aromas and touch, can be so familiar they awaken memory in the body and mind.

My partner, Donny, is a classically trained violinist and violist. In his work of ecstasy and healing he has started playing what he calls "The Concerto for Oneness." Stepping out of his classical training and discarding sheet music, he allows the energies of Spirit to guide the notes he plays in an improvisatory style. Regularly, in our Reiki Healing clinics, he plays spontaneous sounds on his violin or viola as a prayer over the client and practitioner offering Reiki. The sound of Donny's playing is simply another channel for the energetic transfer of Reiki, augmenting the flow that the practitioner creates through the hands.

Donny, in his own organization called Healing Notes (www.healingnotes.org) often goes to Alzheimer's residential care units to play his violin. Often, as he plays Celtic tunes or especially children's music, residents who seldom speak may become animated and begin singing along. Memory awakens and a moment of joy returns through the remembering of the body.

Within Flesh and Spirit community, a monthly drumming circle is held. The rhythm develops as men who may know nothing about drumming begin to express themselves. The research on this shamanistic drumming style is being looked at by holistic hospital care settings as offering some healing benefit. Tone, sound, music are vibrational and may create an atmosphere for ecstatic and healing work. The ancients knew these things and maybe we are just remembering their wisdom.

Aromas

The sense of smell is a powerful tool like music and sound. Essential oils hold benefits such as : awakening memory or association; carrying a vibration from the flower or plant that they are connected to and the power of ancient rituals of anointing that hold their own archetypal connection. (A few essential oil combinations are suggested in the postscript for use specifically to enhance the intention of calling forth each of the six ecstatic archetypes found in Erotic Body Prayer.)

Environmental sensitivities require checking in with receivers about allergies, etc. People with severe immune deficiencies or asthma may be challenged by aromas (incense, smudge or essential oils) thus, making agreements that support healing are necessary.

There are many factors that contribute to environmental diseases being experienced by growing numbers of people today. Not everyone is up to managing, desensitizing or improving their receptivity to aromas, nor do they need to be. However, since aromas hold such healing potential and because they are so present in our modern day world, I might suggest trying behavioral management and hypnotherapy work as a consideration for those challenged by aroma use. (Consult your physician or health care practitioner about such a consideration.)

Certain smells, like certain music, invoke in me associations I have had in this lifetime or possibly even others. Using smells that produce desirable feelings can increase healing in one's body. Like all living things, plants and flowers have their own vibration or sound frequency. Thus, using specific essential oils many activate various energy systems in the body supporting healing. Finally, the ritual of anointing for healing is ancient and can be found in almost all tribes or religious venues. Anointing with an intention enhances one's prayer, engaging the body in the process.

The chemistry of one's body is a product of all the ingredients brought into it. Foods, fluids, air (oxygen/carbon dioxide), chemicals, microorganisms and thoughts create the body smells exuded through the skin. Body smells may offer coded information that may speak to one's mood, health or wellness.

Finally, smells may also indicate external energies influencing the environment. I once met with a channeler who claimed her guide was St. Teresa who was known for bringing roses. In the reading I did with this woman, I experienced a profound healing with my deceased father which concluded with rushes of energy running up and down my spine and the fragrance of roses filling the room.

Similarly, I knew a woman mystic who discerned illness by smells of sulfur. After discerning the smell, she would offer an energetic blessing over the person's body, often producing a feeling of wellness or an actual physical healing. Consider the possibility of using smells to create an environment for healing, to act as a diagnostic tool or offer a sense of spiritual activity as you do ecstatic work.

Ecstatic Movement

As queer folk, dance has been a setting for many to come together. Michael, in Flesh and Spirit, once said to me, "Dance with other queer men is going to church for me." Circuit parties with all their shadowy aspects have been where many queer men have connected to their bodies and experienced a tribal ecstasy that seems very ancient.

When intention and ritual are brought to these experiences of movement and dance, the power and connection in community and the magic is intensified. The use of the body to pray is becoming widespread, with the emergence of Techno Masses with Matthew Fox, 5Rhythms/Sweat Your Prayers with Gabrielle Roth, sacred raves, and TranceDances.

In Flesh and Spirit Community, Mark Peterson and Reed Waller have created a number of Ecstatic Dance Rituals. On retreat, this experience was done naked as we honored our ancestors in ritual. Movement was the primary ingredient in a ritual that culminated in Erotic Body Prayer.

Body Paints, Masks, and Tattoos

Tribal peoples throughout history have painted their bodies, masked themselves or applied sacred images to their bodies. These external acts depict an internal state being drawn out, affirmed, or invoked by spirit.

In the Elder workshop of Flesh and Spirit, we go through an intimate process of creating a plaster mask on a brother while he lays on the floor/blanket naked. Two men carefully apply Vaseline to his face and tissue to areas over eyes and facial hair. They then caringly apply strips of plaster of Paris to his face. Such tender attention creates a unique connection between the men. While the mask is setting on the brother's face, the two mask makers then begin to lightly pleasure this man's body with caressing touch. The intention is to awaken his erotic energy and infuse the mask on his face with that creative force. When the mask has hardened, it is carefully lifted off the brother's face acknowledging his eldership. The mask then is a sacred object, talisman of power and remembrance of who he is.

Body painting can be ecstatic. My partner and I, one day before our wedding, had all of our friends come over to paint our bodies with henna. We chose imagery from a tarot card image 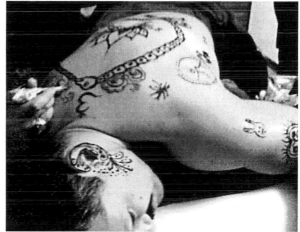 called "the World" as the theme of our wedding The symbology of an Ouroboros or wreath encircles the figure (on the card) as a gateway to a rebirth. This henna tattoo became a ritual blessing for the community to place on our bodies as a spell of our rebirth together. Henna washes away in a couple weeks, unlike permanent tattoos. This is not an encouragement for anyone to get a tattoo. The personal nature of this body art may be as significant as changing your name; you wear it with great deliberateness.

My wondering is about ecstatic expression. Tattoos have become increasingly popular and trendy, yet what meanings do they hold?

I am sure if one took a random sample of Queer folk with tattoos you would find as many reasons as people for the tattoos. However, my non-researched observations have noticed what seems like a theme in the symbology appearing on Queer bodies these days. My philosophical musing asks "is this an expression

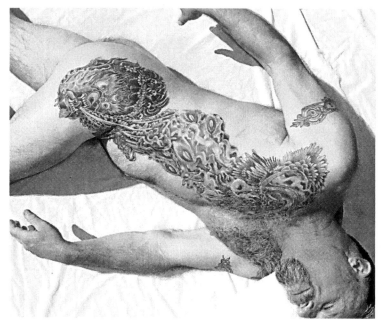

from within or without?"

This Queer brother's story captured all the components for me of the sacred prostitute and midwife of the dying. Here's what it means to him:

I am a man living with AIDS for over 20 years. I have danced with Death throughout that time as I tended to dying friends. I have contemplating my own death as I lay seriously ill. As a result, Death has been a great teacher for me. My tattoo tells my story. In the tattoo, Yama, the Hindu lord of Death, takes the form of a sacred bull and blasts out men's bodies engulfed in flames. The men are erect showing their full sexual power. Yama's hand holds a sacred phallus dripping blood. Out of the burning bodies of the men emerges a phoenix. It has been transformed by erotic energy and death into a new state of being.[9]   Curt

Flogging

Heightened sensation moves one into altered space. Guided flogging has been used as a technique to experience the ecstatic through the body. Allen Siewert has facilitated several ecstatic rituals with flogging for Flesh and Spirit. Even with men for whom this technique has no erotic appeal and with men who were extremely anxious about the process, the experience again provided another tool for awareness, pleasure, or, what may be surprising to some, a connection to the Divine . Some Islamic and Christian sects have used flogging or mortification of the flesh to create altered states and to commune with God.

The scientific community has shown interest in flogging as a practice in pain management benefits, because the process releases endorphins into the bloodstream. So what appears painful to an outside observer may actually reduce pain and free locked muscular holding patterns. Thus, the scientific community is curious to apply this ritual knowledge to those who suffer with chronic pain.

My inclusion of flogging in this compilations of ecstatic techniques is simply to acknowledge it can be used in a manner that is not demeaning, power over another, or even about pain. Among all the vehicles I have noted in this work, this has the least personal appeal, yet I also recognize it to be a tool to awaken a trance-like state that avails one to experience of Spirit through the body.

Laughter

Laughter seems like the perfect closure to a chapter on the Simple Steps for Erotic Body Prayer. Laughter has often been the closing experience to a profound journey with Spirit. After a 13-day fast, I broke into full belly-laughter with a group of people praying for over a half an hour. Waves of kundalini washed through each of us. Following many rebirthing breath-work experiences and ecstatic massage experiences, I have burst into moments of laughter, joy, ecstasy, grief and Samadhi*

In the heart of the AIDS years, I brought together a national conference called AIDS: Living in Recovery. Elisabeth Kübler-Ross spoke, stirring people's stories of grief, unfinished business and then laughter. JoAnn Loulan spoke on sexual healing, awakening participants' consciousnesses while getting them laughing. Presenter after presenter whose words were not funny seemed to well up waves of laughter. The presenter who evoked the direct path was Annette Goodheart, laughter therapist. She pulled people up on stage with her who were very sick, who had almost died or were caregivers of very ill people. Annette's whole teaching was to laugh for no reason. Not because something was funny, but just to laugh. Moments after having people on stage with her, she would ask a few questions about their health and before you knew it, they were laughing uncontrollably.

Another story she told was of the tradition of an African tribe during a funeral. Painting the picture Annette shared, these people believe the spirit is no longer in the body of the deceased, but has traveled on. So a part of the ceremony of the dead as he/she is being carried away off through the hills to the cremation site, is to drop the body along the way. Of course, the crowd who had lost many friends and lovers roared with laughter as she told the story. The playfulness of approaching the body as in the African tribe story seemed to uncork the grief in the room with joyful relief.[10]

In Flesh and Spirit Community, a retreat called *Ecstatic*

Gatekeepers: Conversations with our Ancestors is held to connect to the dead. We construct a manikin-like figure called "the friend" to represent our ancestors. As we carry the "the friend," we make sure we drop him along the way to the fire.

Annette's own story was she has a chronic condition of low blood pressure and she could easily die if her blood pressure was not raised regularly. So, she began using laughter as a way to raise her blood pressure and give her energy to live.

Laughter, as Annette and people like Norman Cousins reported over the years,[#?] changes the body chemistry. It acts as an internal organ massage with many benefits. It is an emotional balancer and I believe clears our energy fields of clutter momentarily.

In my years of being a psychotherapist, I spent a number of years doing sex therapy with couples. So much of the work had to do with getting couples to find what pleasured them without a performance expectation. Although I don't know of any studies to validate this, I was aware couples who had fun, played together and laughed together seemed to enter into increased functioning more easily. Laughter clears the pathways in the physical and energetic bodies so the erotic experience flows without struggle.

In summary, I would say laughter is allowing oneself to lose control. Ecstasy is not a controlled experience. Pleasure is not a controlled experience. Healing is not a controlled experience. When laughter flavors our journey, we may be praying our most authentic prayer. It is a prayer through the body that lubricates our joy and potential for erotic creative juices to flow.

Laugh hardily and heartily!

Dreams

We can chose to open to the ecstatic experience through methods of touch, breathwork, sound, movement, aromas, erotic rituals and laughter. Yet, we can not determine our dreams.

The choice with dreams is to prepare for them. Although we can influence them, ultimately the material of our dreams is managed by something deeper than our cognitive conscious mind.

I add dreams to this list of ways of praying because they are ways in which we meet with ourselves and each other intimately beyond our sense of control.

A friend of mine who is a witch and who taught me much about women's spirituality shares with me about women who live together who menstruate around the same time. "The connection of being in each other's energy often shifts each other's menstrual cycles when they live together," she said. The same principal often influences our dream life. When we hold the intention that our dreams are speaking, not only for the individual, but for the community, it is so.

Flesh and Spirit Community has facilitated a number of dream circles. We would prepare the circle by reviewing dreams together and using gestalt Exercises to dramatize dreams we had had already. Using this Jungian idea that each person, place or thing in our dreams represented a part of ourselves, we gave voice to aspects of our dreams that were often illuminating.

After working with past dreams to get comfortable with dream work, we then would do an erotic ritual and visualization to guide us into our sleep time.

The erotic ritual of being naked, touching and connecting with each man in circle allowed the metaphor of being vulnerable and power to flow into our dream circle. We prepared our sleeping circle so each man's head faced the center of the circle and closed with a visualization weaving each man's heart story together as we went into dream time.

At one dream circle in Flesh and Spirit, sometimes humorously referred to as "orchestrated snoring circles," we all drifted into states of beta and theta brain waves, the waves that occur when someone is meditating or in a trance state. Each man, even those who almost never dream, dreamed. The dreams came in epic stories or fragments. Yet, just dreaming together seemed to deepen our intimacy with each other.

The richness our dream circles took us as a community into a deeper awareness of how intimate our connections are. Often, common, shared images would emerge, or themes that seemed to tie our dreams together would emerge. Winged ones, winged men, birds and serpents have often appeared in our dreaming together. Flesh and Spirit Community created our logo of the feathered serpent* from shared dreams.

From these circles, we found each time we went on a retreat together it was valuable to collect our dreams, to listen to the themes of healing, visioning and instruction from Spirit that came from this. Now, when we go on retreat, we encourage men to begin

---

feathered serpent bringers of ancestral medicine, bearers of peace and hope infused the community with a deeper sense of new tribal consciousness.

journaling their dreams beforehand, knowing the information begins to emerge for healing and inspiration. Like women whose cycles blend together, so our dreaming becomes one dream.

Our exchange of energy changes our consciousness collectively, much like the chemistry of women's bodies blend together in menstruation. This blending of our body's information through the vibration of unheard sounds creates an environment for shared dreaming and a sense of bonding in community.

The potential from dreaming together may be to rewrite our old body stories anew. In community, we may have the opportunity to recreate the stories that were energetically encoded through the family or cultural environments we grew up in. In our families, most of us slept in close proximity to each other. Thus, our sleep times were filled with the energetics of each person's story in the family. Dreaming together in loving community with the intention of each person's highest good can assist in reprogramming the story to wholeness.

All material creates a sound frequency. Each organ, tissue and cell of our bodies have individual and collective sounds.

In a recent dream, I had prior to a Flesh and Spirit retreat, I heard a voice saying, "You are citizens of the reconstruction." In the dream my partner and I were inviting men from Flesh and Spirit to go around the world and create sacred circles announcing, "You are citizens of the reconstruction."

The depth and breath of these words have yet to reveal themselves. The impact of these words began a depth of conversation in our community that is echoing in our bodies and minds as a community. This dream seems to be stirring a curiosity in us as we continue to remember and redefine who we are in community now. The fact that you are reading this book may be a part of actualizing this dream.

Many times one may not be able to dream in close proximity to another's physicality and thus not in close proximity to their dense energetic field surrounding them. In such instances, you can make contracts to share in common dream space with an intention. Choose a time period, if possible, to make that connection, even if you are across the world from the individual or community you wish to dream with. One person or community might be in meditation while the other person or community is in a sleep state. These potential beta and theta states combined with ritual and intention create a clear link for information to be shared. (If you are Reiki-attuned, you may wish to add the Hon Sha Ze Sho Nen to this transfer of love). Dream together.

All the ecstatic tools and techniques shared in this section are ways of touching each other, creating intimacy and changing the world. Whenever possible, step into each other's energy fields, so your armor can be dismantled and the illusion of separation can be dispelled. Step into each other's energy field praying through your body for the wholeness of the earth.

Any of these techniques that have been described may accentuate your ability to have an ecstatic experience of praying through your body.

H. Agreement and Gratitude

I confess I find more ecstasy in passion

than in prayer. Such passion is prayer. I

confess I pray still to feel the touch of my

lover's lips, his hands upon me, his arms

enfold me. Such surrender has been mine.

I confess I hunger to still be filled and

inflamed, to melt into the dream of us.

Beyond this troubled place to where we are

not even ourselves, to know that always this

is mine. [11]

Veronica Franco
Sixteenth century courtesan tried by the Inquisition for witchcraft.

Confess to one another and pray for one

another that you may be healed. [12]

James 5:16 Revised Standard Version

During the New Testament era when the words of the apostle James were compiled, the term "confession" was translated as an agreement—an intention. The term "sin" could be translated as missing the mark as an archer. These translations invite us to regard our human imperfections with great compassion—not only for ourselves, but for others, and for entire communities.

Such compassion is an essential element of Erotic Body Prayer. Both partners in healing agree to work together on the issues and wounds they wish to heal. Of course, there will be times when either or both partners may feel that they have missed the mark, or felt somehow victimized by others who have missed the mark.

Once more, as we move into healing journeys, the process is not always about our own "sins," wounds or patterns, but about the larger wounds of our communities. Our people, the ancestors of our families, our ancestors as a queer people, queer men, or any tribal group to which we belong may become a part of our confession or our intention of healing. Our erotic lives are deeply influenced by our personal and communal histories; discovering this unity through ecstatic bodywork often opens a wonderful invitation in our hearts to heal our own wounds.

For many years in my practice as a psychotherapist, I used hypnosis with my clients. In hypnosis, clients would experience an altered state where a "suggestion" could be introduced into their consciousness to support them in their goal. In Erotic Body Prayer, the many ways of touching create an altered state that allows the desired intention to be taken into the "mind of the body." With compassion and awareness, we become better archers, and better keepers of agreements, not only in bodywork, but in our lives.

Agreement and Healing Partnerships

Before completing this book it was important to me to experience Erotic Body Prayer fully as a receiver. Thus, I asked a friend who is a psychologist to do several sessions of this method of prayer with me. After teaching him the basics, which he knew intuitively already, he did work with me.

My intention was clear as I embarked on a series of sessions with my psychologist friend. I wanted to heal my eyes. I have a cataract in my right eye, impairing my vision even with corrective lenses, and my left eye is blind from a surgical procedure that was meant to remove a cataract from that eye.

Also, as I disclosed earlier in my writing, I am a sexual abuse survivor. My abuse by my father was brief and angry, and was followed by comfort and affection. My body story was deeply encoded with pan and comfort being linked together.

For years my eyes have been my guides to inner healing work with clients who are facing conditions like cancer, HIV and other chronic manageable diseases.

These sessions followed up on some work I had done years before with "Dr. Mel," a western physician who used his Native American spirituality in healing work. Dr. Mel asked me to enter into a dialogue with my cataracts as if they were living entities. I asked my cataracts, "Why are you here?" I also asked them, "How are you serving me?" I experienced the answer that came back as much with my body as with my mind. My cataracts said, "We're here to protect you from a world you didn't want to see." These words have led me through many journeys of self-healing prior to the start of my own Erotic Body Prayer sessions with my psychologist friend.

Our sessions were filled with the techniques described in this manual. During each session, I would have him lay his hands over my eyes and offer me healing energy, and we would listen to the information we both picked up from our bodies.

In one of the sessions I wished to welcome my father into this healing journey. I asked my psychologist friend to be his conduit of healing. This time, it was me asking my father (as personified by my friend) to hold me and share erotic pleasure with me. This reenactment of pleasure without pain, combined with emotional safety and mutual agreements, allowed me to experience yet another piece of healing. Since then, I have experienced some improvement in the frequency and levels of cloudiness of my vision. My eyes are not "fixed", but from our sessions I have gained more hope that I will be able to manage my condition, until or if there should be further physical improvement.

Gratitude

As in any spiritual practice, gratitude is an essential part of closure. It is always important to honor the spirit of celebration, rest and empowerment that we share in our healing work. Experiencing gratitude takes us out of the realm victimization, and into the realm of the survivor. Gratitude is the experience of being alive and integrated in flesh and spirit.

Share your gratitude with your partner in recognition of your experience together. Whether your experience of Erotic Body Prayer brings up a sense of work, pleasure, love, pain, or transformation, take the time to offer yourself and your partner gratitude for simply being there.

As you allow the integration of flesh and spirit, the words of Rumi that were invoked in the introduction to this manual may begin to have greater meaning: "If you want to know how Jesus raised the dead, kiss me on the lips."[13] I believe Rumi is suggesting that the transformative power of love goes beyond all other forces in its capacity to heal; our only real work is to learn how to relax into love, and to allow the spiral dance of energy it creates within our bodies.

The power to resurrect yourself, the queer community and the world around you can be shared and affirmed in your touch, your caresses, and your kisses. Kiss passionately. Kiss deeply. So be it.

VII. Postscript:
A Developing Community

The concepts, principles and practices laid out in this book, *Erotic Body Prayer,* have been the foundation of the work I have shares in my private practice but profoundly magnified in Flesh and Spirit Community.

Some basic observations of using the erotic as a thread of weaving a queer men's spiritual community together.

Internal and External Forces

If as many teachers of spirit suggest our outer world is an out-picturing of our inner world, then I must take responsibility for my experience completely and fully. Following that thinking, as we engage in community, the community has the opportunity to grow from the mirror of that out-picturing in its total experience. The men in that community have the opportunity of knowing themselves and facing their fears, in the safety and support of what they have created together. The Peaceful Warrior is the foundation stone upon which we can build community.

I have a long history of beginning and constructing communities. In my youth, I helped form an ecumenical charismatic community where the model of living in communal households was the attempt to hold together an intimate sharing of love and purpose.

When I became a psychotherapist, I ran numerous groups that ran for 8 years. With the appearance of AIDS, I co-facilitated a Healing Circle for 9 years. As an activist, I was President of the Gay, Lesbian, Bisexual, Transgender Alliance. Each of these expe-

159

riences helped shape my ideas of the magic of communities. Flesh and Spirit started in 1992.

What I have learned about myself and community in the process of Flesh and Spirit's development is yet another book. However, here are a few things I have learned:

- To laugh
- To love my weaknesses and mistakes and ask for help
- To hold a vision without being attached to the outcome
- The law of attraction is true. My work is to have compassion for myself as I clear and re-wire my body-stories with my intentions. In community, the law of attraction magnifies.
- To allow and accept people with the grace to come and go
- To free myself of judgements that even if a person is clear about their truth (in any given moment) the picture being presented is often not complete. Everything is in change.
- To recognize I am ultimately my only judge, so be free of approval.
- To listen with all aspects of my mind, my body and my spirit, while affirming I am doing the best I can with the knowledge and understanding I have.
- All feelings are valid and I choose my feelings to align with my highest intention.
- Some internal work we do does come to completion.
- Love never fails.
- I am never alone. In community, I know this (when

fear has not seized my attention)
- Whatever shows up is perfect.
- There is no lack in myself and there is no lack in community. What is available is wholeness.
- We are powerful beyond our conscious imagining.
- We can do more (internally and externally) for ourselves and the world in community.
- Community may be the hope of the new world, no matter how the political, social, economic and religious winds of change may blow.
- Community is the ultimate vision of oneness that we can live in now.
- If we're not having fun, we're missing something.
- We are never alone.

A Culture of Influence

It is also my belief we internalize the culture around us to some degree energetically. Some of that internalization happens because there are still body stories that need attention, healing, compassion or re-wiring. There is often an energetic vulnerability in our fields, especially when we feel less than powerful.

The work of Flesh and Spirit began in Cincinnati, Ohio, as I have mentioned earlier. The container for this ancient/new and pioneering work was born in an environment predominantly culturally conservative, a climate where gay oppression had thrived. Internally, homophobia was overt and subtle among many queer people in the city. It was the perfect place to raise up a holistic approach to spirituality and eroticism. The hunger for affirmative models seemed to be great and yet the split of the old stories of "all and none thinking" seemed to be at work (even if cloaked) in the most advanced thinkers of the gay movement, and certainly present in the "average" queer person coming out.

Thus, many men doing Flesh and Sprit work in Cincinnati would have transformative experiences that were often invalidated by the broad culture and in turn in the gay culture of the time.

For those who might be reading this from places similar to Cincinnati, I would offer you more encouragement than I felt in those initial years. You most probably would not be reading this book if you had not already begun a significant spiritual journey that hold the erotic as sacred. Plus, the increasing exposure to this kind of work is more widely recognized in the queer culture. And finally, I would offer there are ways of doing spiritual work over geographic locations that may enhance the possibilities of gathering this kind of consciousness together in community.

The San Francisco Bay Area is, of course, a unique place for queer spirituality and erotic spirituality to flourish It is a crucible for free thinking to be expressed. The work of Flesh and Spirit has been one of many voices and options for queer men to explore.

In this more fertile field, however, my observations for growth call for two scary-sounding words: discipline (in practice) and commitment.

The beauty of San Francisco is that it has a bit of everything for the spiritual seeker and also much for the pursuer of the erotic. In this container with so many options, the seeker often goes to everything and often belongs to numerous communities. Thus, many exciting and transformative experiences are spread across many people or a number of groups. This web-weaving may enhance one's journey while at times it may serve as a way to not be fully intimate (seen and known) by any one community.

Similarly, I reject the notion that repeating a workshop,

retreat, ritual or practice need necessarily result in "been there, done that." Mystical traditions invite one into practices that require discipline and repetition to go deeper. My advocacy as I open this observation about building community is that one should only practice something because it brings one joy or freedom or it opens one's heart.

Stage Processes of Community

This notion of being intimately a part of a community may be new to some of you, or the wounds of past experiences in community may cause hesitance to consider such a prescription for your future. I would ask you to consider community in its meanings for your own enhanced process of being your full potential. When the agenda becomes something else it is the saboteur's dream of disillusionment.

A s a psychotherapist I learned some three-stage models for the progress of an individual's relationship with a community.[1] Model I suggests in relationship(s) we often enter a community and discover **Magic**: "Wow, I've found something special."

Following the initial magic, the individual's relationship with the community humanizes. The community becomes more human and therefore fallible. This stage is **Disillusionment**. The model held that as we express our feelings of Disillusionment, we can choose to come into a more balanced state of simultaneous magic and disillusionment, which the author calls **Mystery**.

The Mystic Rumi describes an ecstatic journey as to ability to hold the beauty of magic and disillusionment, for then you can see yourself as the beloved and the face of God. The intimacy of community seems to require this of me, of us.

The other process from my graduate training was a group

dynamic in three stages. The stages move from **Inclusion**, where one feels like one belongs, to **Control,** where power is challenged because one no longer feels included, and finally to **Affection**, the stage one gets to harmoniously if one takes back the power to feel included.

One of the beauties of being in a community that often sweats its prayers together is to observe these processes of magic and dis-illusionment turn to mystery and the issues that arise through control diminish as the felt experience of belonging takes root over time.

Queer theologian, Carter Hayward has been quoted saying, "our work is not to see only who is in the circle, but who is not."[2] Flesh & Spirit is ever expanding its inclusiveness of men who love men seeking an ecstatic path.

Among Flesh & Spirit Community we inhabit bodies:

Young (from twenties)
Older (to seventies)
bodies of all colors and racial tribes
bodies surviving HIV or AIDS and healthy bodies that
share the challenge of HIV
bodies with cancer and healthy bodies that share the
challenge of cancer.
sighted bodies and partially non-sighted bodies
hearing bodies and partially non-hearing bodies
bodies in recovery from drugs, alcohol, eating & sex dis-
orders, internalized homophobia,
sexism, racism, and gender bias.

*Bodies that grew up in love and bodies that grew up with
experiences of verbal, physical
and sexual abuse.
Tattooed, pierced and ritualized body art and bodies
without additive markings
surgically enhanced bodies and bodies non-altered,
hairy bodies and smooth bodies
scarred bodies and non-scarred bodies
bodies of pleasure with varied genitals of shape, size and
function
short bodies and tall bodies
fully mobile bodies and partially mobile bodies
large bodies and lean bodies
muscular bodies and soft tissue bodies
bodies with large energy and bodies with close energy
bodies of individual fragrances and chemistries
bodies of emotional variability
bodies attuned to outer world and
bodies attuned to inner world
bodies with wide variability of sensory awareness
bodies that are celibate except in sacred space
bodies that are sexually active seeking a partner
bodies that are sexually active, web weaving without a
desire for partnership
bodies that are polyamorous*

So far Flesh & Spirit has welcomed four transgendered brothers, yet only one is at the core of the community. There have been
a number of men of color in Flesh and Spirit. However, the ratio
is small. Our inclusiveness welcomes men of all economic ranges,

however currently there are few men who are financially affluent among our members.

Creating an inclusive community is not a forced action, but an internal process of opening one's heart space, clearing any exclusive stories of fears, prejudices and judgments about difference. A willingness to examine ourselves through the lens of who is present and who is not may guide us in our future steps of becoming our mission statement of love.

I grew up as a teenager hearing the words of Jesus being preached, "Be perfect as your heavenly father is perfect." This imperative seemed like an unattainable goal. Yet, when these words are translated from the Aramaic or Greek, one finds a Queer message and the message central to Flesh and Spirit Community: inclusiveness. One Aramaic meaning my teacher, Sri Ronji, shared for the word "perfect" is "inclusive." Be inclusive as the cosmic universe, the Divine Mother and Father, are inclusive. Another meaning from the Greek text for "perfect" is "mature." Be mature as the Source is mature.

As all our communities become more inclusive and developmentally mature and the Queer movement finds wholeness, our gifts will abound for all. My visions and the visions of Flesh and Spirit Community have encompassed this notion of inclusiveness through the idea of creating sanctuaries, especially for Queer folk, who are often left out in their growth and development.

In a time when "homeland security" and "broken borders" are constant buzz phrases and the label "evil" is used to create a greater separation from understanding, the need for sanctuaries is increasing.

Sanctuary allows a safe space for one to heal and take full responsibility for one's own life with more ease. San Francisco,

Flesh and Spirit's home, has been sanctuary for gay immigrants for decades. The words of Harvey Milk, San Francisco's first gay city supervisor said in a speech before his assassination:

> I can't forget the looks on faces of people who've lost hope. Be they gay, be they seniors, be they blacks looking for an almost impossible job, be they Latins trying to explain their problems and aspirations in a tongue that's foreign to them. I personally will never forget that people are more important than buildings. I use the word I because I'm proud. I stand here tonight in front of gay sisters and brothers because I'm proud of you. I think it is time we have legislators who are gay and proud of the fact and do not have to stay in the closet. I think that a gay person, up-front, will not walk away from responsibility and be afraid of being tossed out of office. After Dade County, I walked among the angry and the frustrated night after night and I looked at their faces. And in San Francisco, three days before Gay Pride Day, a person was killed just because he was gay. And that night, I walked among the sad and the frustrated at City Hall in San Francisco and later that night as they lit candles on Castro Street and stood in silence, reaching out for some symbolic thing that would give them hope. These were strong people, people whose faces I knew from the shop, the streets, meetings and people who I had never saw before but I knew. They were strong, but they needed hope.
>
> And the young gay people in the Altoona, Pennsylvanias and the Richmond, Minnesotas who are coming out and hear Anita Bryant on television and her story. The only thing they have to look forward to is hope. And you have to give them hope. Hope for a better world, hope for better tomorrow, hope for a better place to come to if the pressures at home are too great. Hope that all will be alright.

> Without hope, not only the gays, but the blacks, the seniors,
> the handicapped, the us'es, the us'es will give up. And if you
> help elect to the central committee and other offices, more
> gay people, that gives a green light to all who feel disenfran-
> chised, a green light to move forward. It means hope to a
> nation that has given up, because if a gay person makes it,
> the doors are open to everyone.
>   So if there is a message I have to give, it is that if
> I've one overriding thing about my personal election, it's the
> fact that if a gay person can be elected, it's a green light. And
> you and you, and you have to give people hope.[3]

I am sure Harvey Milk understood the only true sanctuary is within ourselves. In our bodies is the true homeland security and in our energy field is the one real border to welcome or redirect the energies of others. Having said that, creating outer sanctuaries to optimize the potential for wholeness is an ecstatic mission. A place where one can choose with ease the wholeness one wishes to embrace and the free expression of one's gifts is the experience of sanctuary. Stepping out of being a victim to hope builds sanctuary.

Environments such as San Francisco or Amsterdam offer a level of felt safety that is external, allowing the internal reality of safety to become actualized in one's body. In these environments, the cognitive dissonance that one may have internalized from oppressive environments has a chance to heal as one chooses to live a new story of freedom. The work, then, of the ecstatic seeker is to acknowledge safety in oneself as one gathers like-minded peo- ple of safety together in community whether in San Francisco like Flesh and Spirit or in the Midwest of the United State, Egypt, Afghanistan or the place in which you live.

These Queer "holy places" are sanctuary, yet they do not heal us alone. "Geographic cures," as spoken of in 12-step work, are not the answer, for one brings who one is to each location. I am my own sanctuary as I am one with my true nature.

The statistics around Queer people in open (or less oppressed) environments may indicate more wholeness, but it is clear that sanctuary itself does not cure. Estimates of the GLBT population in San Francisco are around 30%*. HIV sero-conversion rates have gone down in the past five years* (2001–2006) and yet drug addiction among queer folk may remains high or higher than in the past.

Safe places for any oppressed group allow them to choose healing, recovery and wholeness with ease. As political fundamentalists create an atmosphere of oppression and repression around race, religion, gender, sex, sexual orientation, economic status and physical abilities, sanctuaries will be essential models of equality that all marginalized peoples will need.

Prophetically, I would challenge us as a Queer folk to hold a vision where we no longer need oppression to push us into action. Imagine a Queer president of the United States (or any county of the world). Imagine Queer spirituality and Queer spiritual leaders forging dialogue and peace talks. Imagine commercials that would commonly depict happy, whole Queer consumers. Imagine Queer healers from every discipline being honored as contributors in breakthroughs in science, medicine, environment, justice, poverty, disease, education, arts and family.

Innovative communities like Flesh and Spirit have unique opportunities to raise the level of safety and thus sanctuary so visions of the above might shine forth. If all the Queer folk of the world would come out about their sacred bodies, their sacred relationships, their sacred erotic energy, the world would not remain blind. The antidote for radical fundamentalism may be the creation and visibility of communities that touch skin, open hearts and raise spirits. If the scales of balance have tipped too far, then our contribution as visible ecstatic communities may assist the necessary shift in the world's consciousness.

Volumes could be written about each year of Flesh and Spirit Community since its inception in 1992. Yet, just for stirring the creative forces of the development process I wrote down a
word or two to describe the process I saw going on in its development. If you are a member of Flesh and Spirit, or any community you might try this exercise to assist you in developing a vision/strategies to go further.

1992 Risk-taking
1993 Adventure
1994 Stability
1995 Dreaming
1996 Transition
1997 Seeding
1998 Optimism
1999 Growth
2000 Peak
2001 Community
2002 Refocus
2003 Expansion
2004 Disillusion/mystery
2005 Challenge/detachment
2006 Re-vision
2007 (what word would you like to describe this stage?)

The tone or vibration of each stage of Flesh and Spirit's (or any organization's) development sends out an energetic message of attraction. Each person's body has an energy field pulsating out into the world. The stories contained in that energy activates the law of attraction. The law of attraction offers back in like kind whatever intentions have been projected out through words, actions and energy. This same principle is true of a group, community, organization or a nation.

Considering this principle during any given time in a community's development may offer some insight into the messages being energetically created by the overall membership of that community. The themes you might describe for any given year are then mirrored by the kinds of members attracted to join and stay within the community.

Observing what kind of men joined Flesh and Spirit during this year of re-visioning offers clues of understanding. Again, if you are a member of Flesh and spirit or any community, what has the new membership said to you as a mirror? Also, what has the reamaining and sustaining membership said by staying? The Law of Attraction is ever speaking to us through what is present.

When I mused about both the sustaining members and the new members joining Flesh and Spirit Community, almost all were men going through some significant re-definition, e.g. death of a mother or father, change of partnership, start partnership, career/vocational shift, financial shifts, becoming a visible leader, moved home, and broadened their volunteerism/service. All these personal experiences as well as the sweeping free of Flesh and Spirit's home to the fire make it easy to applaud to this stage of development. Use this process to bring grace to your appreciation of the communities you are choosing to build.

The law of attraction always applies. Thus, if someone or something is not present, it is a reflection of where you and the community are in your process. This is not a judgment. inclusiveness is an internal position of heart. If you and your community are in an open hearted space, then celebrate what is there, while being available to what may show up to expand the circle. Allow sanctuary to be a space for you first, then you will have room for others.

If this thinking has any meaning, the observation of the kind of men who have joined Flesh and Spirit Community in this period of re-visioning is curious. Consistent with my own desire for Flesh and Spirit, the new men often have done some significant work on themselves to come into what appears to be a teaching community. Yet, another observation of this past year is how many of these men have been in significant processes of re-definition, which often took them to other paths/choices (which may or may not weave back into significant participation of Flesh and Spirit).

Core Process

The path of ecstasy and healing through community may look like this:

The core of men in Flesh & Spirit Community seem to be on a journey that includes this cycle. It has clearly been my process. Beginning as student (gathering whatever apprenticeships available to become the teacher), I now find myself teaching everything I know as mentor so others can teach and broaden the circle.It is said,"as we heal, we heal others" As the men of Flesh & Spirit heal, they seem to lead as they are ready, deepening that healing which may only come from teaching what one knows. This cycle is based on humility, for we all remain students of mastery.

Understanding these processes may allow the grace to move through these stages ensuring the outcomes to be free and the next stage of potential to emerge. Thus, being clear about who you are and what your intention is, is essential.

How many times have you, how many times have I, joined a group of community and find at some point it doesn't fit any

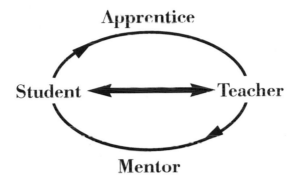

longer. Before fleeing to the next community, check in with yourself about what body story may be emerging for you to heal.

A very dear soul came to Flesh and Spirit Community to join our heartful space to feel included/belong, in a place where the body/erotic and sprit were integrated. In the intake interview, he spoke clearly of how he had felt invalidated and unheard by leaders in other communities. This awareness popped up for him after we had done an intimate touch exercise and he was asked to step back/away. In the stepping back he felt rejected even though he was simple following the instruction of the exercise. We noted this important body story in the interview as he was welcomed into the community to attend the Peaceful Warrior workshop the following week.

In The Peaceful Warrior workshop, this brother was guided to do a pushing exercise that is not pleasant, to open his body to the stories around "dealing with conflict heartfully." Each step of this exercise is carefully set up to provide a safe and sacred space for healing to take place. As one might expect, his story of feeling rejected emerged through the pushing exercise. In beginning to offer possible interpretations to this experience about belonging in community, he became enraged. He wished to leave the circle. I asked that he stay to be clear about his leaving and that the other brothers would have a chance to hold his exit compassionately as well. Although he held onto his story energetically in leaving, he was validated for being in his truth even though he was not being rejected but loved by the group. This he could not deny, even though the felt a dissonance.

It was such a clear demonstration for each man in the circle of doing the best he could to shift the old stories carried in their bodies. Many brothers had very powerful breakthroughs that day. Understanding compassion towards old stories is the only way we can heal. Also to accept (as Peaceful Warriors) the reality that creating a healing environment for persons to step into does not always mean they will receive the healing being extended.

Community is a dynamic, not stagnant, so redefining a shared mission and vision regularly is essential. It seems to me as our world globalizes, multiple communities will stand as beacons of light and act as sanctuary for those in less safe or conscious environments. A possible vision I have of Flesh and Spirit is to build a strong intimate community in San Francisco while developing satellite communities around the world. This broad base vision calls for building leaders who are willing to explore a holistic journey of body and spirit with a level of intimacy that may only come over time. Creating safe and sacred space and holding the intention of wholeness is our only responsibility. The final response belongs to each person taking full responsibility for themselves.

Postscript: A Developing Community

Jeremiah 20:9 (New International Version)

But if I say, "I will not mention him

or speak any more in his name,"

his/her word is in my heart like a fire,

a fire shut up in my bones.

I am weary of holding it in;

indeed, I cannot.

What are some of the visions of community you have for yourself?
What is the prophetic message your community adds to usher in
the new consciousness of love for our planet?

Our ancestors ask us to remember who we are. The world
awaits the awakening of the Queer Tribe. Dream Big.

VIII. Archetype Exercises

Use these exercises to strengthen your spiritual and physical immune system. When you are empowered, your body responds in kind. These exercises are designed to engage your exploration through tools for the mind (affirmational) body (oil, activity and yoga posture). Try using a journal to listen to yourself on this ecstatic path.

Following each archetype description, I would invite you to do an affirmation exercise in relationship to each archetype. For those of you who are queer, you might preface the initial statement with the word "queer" and see what appears.

Peaceful Warrior

Looking into a mirror or in your imagination (mind's eye) affirm these statements:

"I am a (queer) Peaceful Warrior." Say it repeatedly until it connects you to a sense of your compassionate and powerful self, or until some self statement or feeling emerges as a response. Notice without judgment.

Take the exercise further by affirming some of the attributes of a peaceful warrior.

Notice which ones resonate in your body and which do not. Allow the information to support your awareness.

I am powerful.

I am compassionate.

I am willing to face my fears.

I am willing to know myself.

I ask for help easily.

I approach conflict heartfully.

I set boundaries that work for me.

I re-set boundaries as I change.

I say "yes" when I mean "yes".

I say "no" when I mean "no".

I am willing to love myself by saying "no.

I am my own authority.

Finally, imagine what you would be like if you could transform all the fears of your life.

Transform might be release or integrate the fears so they no longer inhibit you from the desires of your heart.

Take a moment to activate/seal your affirmation as a Peaceful Warrior by anointing yourself on each chakra with a mixture of lavender essential oil (for calmness/peacefulness), sandalwood and patchouli (for the masculine warrior elements of yourself). You might use these after bathing in the morning, to start your day or before sleep time to empower your dream states. Both are excellent times to absorb the vibration of the essential oil.

Part I
(a version of)
Aikido: New Warrior Exercise

Stand with your feet apart about shoulder length. Rest your hands in front of you. With a large inhalation breath, raise your

hands up in a circular motion over your head to an outstretched, horizontal position, palms facing upwards. Concurrently, step to the side horizontally with one foot and bring a slight bend to the knees. Do this several times until it no longer feels mechanical. Each time, notice the sensations and feelings in your body.

Part II

The alternate exercise from Aikido begins with your feet solidly on the ground. Place your non-dominant hand over your (dantian/hara)(footnote) the area between your 2nd and 3rd chakra) just beneath your belly button. Take a full breath while stepping forward with your dominant foot, thrust your dominant hand out in front of you while exhaling and vocalizing the sound "hut."

Do this several times so it does not feel mechanical. Notice

what feelings and sensations you have in your body.

This exercise frames the work and balance of the peaceful warrior in the world. You need both aspects of the exercise for balance. If one part of the exercise feels more challenging it is the part that needs the most support from you at this time.

This exercise is a read on what your body is putting out energetically not what you may think about your sense of harmony.

Part I often speaks to one's availability, receptivity or "yes" to the world. It may also indicate your openness, especially to compassion towards yourself and the world.

Part II may indicate one's ability to set boundaries, say "no," or extend yourself out into the world. It may also speak to your sense of power and powerfulness to influence your world.

The Peaceful Warrior's power and compassion comes from the intimate knowledge you are one with the earth.

The element of the peaceful warrior is earth. If you are able to be naked on the land, allow yourself to stand like the image of the da Vinci Vitruvian man, pulling the energy up your spine with each breath. With each exhalation allow yourself to release that which you don't need back into the earth. Rituals using the element of the earth will enhance that connection and thus increase one's sense of power and compassion.

If possible, use the element of the earth on your body. A face mask of clay and water is not only a good beauty treatment, but a way to deeply connect to the earth. Even better might be taking whole mud bath. Many spas are set up for the health benefits of such a treatment, and you might take the experience further with the intention of connecting to the earth. A final possible ritual would involve getting help from others to dig a large hole for you to stand or lay down in and then cover your body (except your

head, of course) with soil. This can be powerful medicine and requires cere-monial assis-tants to help you with the experience.

In a consulta-tion once with Malidoma Some, he said, "rituals are meant to take you out of your comfort." Stretch yourself to embrace rituals that work for you, while you are also gentle with yourself for taking any step at all.

Thank the earth for supporting you.

Lover

Looking into a mirror or in your imagination (mind's eye), affirm these statements:

Warrior II
Virabhadrasana II

I am a (queer) lover.
I am willing to integrate the conflicting parts of myself.
I am available to intimacy.
I honor all the relationships of my life no matter how each one felt.
I am willing to release all my grief (that no longer serves my highest good) Finally, imagine what you would be like if you could transform all the grief in your life. Transform might be release or integrate the grief so it no longer inhibits you from the desires of your heart:
I am willing to be totally independent and totally intimate.
I am willing to be true to myself no matter what my "intimates(s)" might want.
I am willing to be equal with my "intimates."

Take a moment to activate and seal your affirmation as a Lover by anointing yourself on each chakra with a mixture of rosemary (remembering/healing), orange blossom and cinnamon (integrating parts of yourself). You might use these after bathing in the morning, to start your day or before sleep time to empower your dream states. Both are excellent times to absorb the vibration of the essential oil. Since water is the element of the lover, consider these ritual exercises to awaken the Lover within you. If using a shower, spend a moment imagining the shower pouring forth healing water. Start your shower by being your own lover of your body. Body gels or soaps that accentuate and awaken your sensations are helpful as you begin exploring every part of your body. Bring your thoughts of appreciation and pleasure to each part, especially the parts you feel less good about. Slow down. This shower is not a function of getting clean, it is a shower to notice and enjoy every muscle, skin texture, hair, nail, organ and skeletal feature unique to your amazing body. Be sure to towel yourself off as lovingly as you caressed your body in the shower.

If you are able to bathe in a tub or pool, you might take the care of being your own lover further. Bubble bath, flowers, the essential oils suggested for anointing, candles, a bit of fruit, chocolate, juice/wine available around you at your finger tips, set an environment of luxury. Begin your exploration again acknowledging every part of your body sensuously with sponge or the silkiness of your hands. The more you pamper yourself, the more you are telling the universe you are available to receive all you desire.

If you have the opportunity to go to a stream, lake or large body of water, allow the spirit of the water to awaken you. This time, I would have you use this natural setting to offer a baptism of blessing on you as a lover. Release what you no longer need to carry and welcome the abundance of love available to you.

Thank the water for supporting you.

Reclining Hero Pose
Supta Virasana

Sacred Prostitute

Looking into a mirror or in your imagination (mind's eye), affirm these statements:

> I am a (queer) sacred prostitute
>
> a sexual healer
>
> a sacred intimate
>
> I am willing to serve through my body without an attachment.
>
> I am willing to give and receive pleasure without attachment.
>
> I am willing to heal myself and thus offer healing to others.
>
> I am willing to release shame (that no longer serves my highest good)
>
> I am an erotic spiritual man.

Finally, imagine what you would be like if you could transform all the shame in your life. Transform might mean release or integrate shame so it no longer inhibits the desires of your heart.

Take a moment to activate and seal your affirmation as a Sacred Prostitute by anointing yourself on each chakra with a mixture of amber and musk (to awaken the sensual and sensory memory of the body). You might use these after bathing in the morning, to start your day or before sleep time to empower your dream states. Both are excellent times to absorb the vibration of the essential oil.

Sit naked with a candle in front of you. Warm your hands with the comfortable flame of the candle. Spread the warmth from your hands over your body. Acknowledge as you touch your body with the fire's warmth, "my sacred body is of service."

Gather props for the ritual of the Sacred Prostitute. Candles, lotion, lubricant, incense and pictures or memorabilia of people you wish to pray for. If you do not have an object that connects you to the persons you wish to direct energy to, then write down their names to make concrete your intention. Surround yourself in a circle of candles, add incense, a symbol of your prayers, and get comfortable on a blanket or bed in the center of the circle. Set your intention that your self-pleasuring will raise the energy of your prayer. Like the Lover caress yourself, playing with your erogenous zones, genitals, nipples, whole body as you send energy to support the highest good of the situation you are praying for. Your pictures, memorabilia or names are inside this circle of awakened energy. If you know Reiki or wish to acknowledge the distance healing mantra, "hon sha ze shon nen," then do so. Affirm your pleasure as it hightens the vibration of your selfless intention of love.

Of course, for those of you who wish to face the fears, shame and stories that inhibit your journey of sacred service with your body, you might consider a fire walk. This is to be done only with certified trained professionals. Until then, imagine a fire walk and your mastery of working with fire to create the world you wish.

Thank the fire for supporting you.

Elder

Looking into a mirror or in your imagination (mind's eye), affirm these statements:

Child's Pose
Adho Mukha Virasana

I am a (queer) elder.

I am a teacher.

I am a mentor.

I am a leader.

I am whole.

I am a facilitator of community.

I am inclusive.

I am just.

I hold all as my equal.

I walk between the worlds.

I take my place in community.

I encourage others to find their place in community.

I hold sacred all things and all parts of myself.

I am willing to release any sense of not belonging.

Finally, imagine what you would be like if you could transform all the feelings/stories of not belonging to fully belonging in all situations.

Take a moment to activate and seal your affirmation as the Elder by anointing yourself on each chakra with a mixture of sage (to ignite the ancient wisdom) and tea tree (to support wholeness). You might use these after bathing in the morning, to start your day or before sleep time to empower your dream states. Both are excellent times to absorb the vibration of the essential oil.

The Elder is an ever-expanding role of teacher and student. The element of air fills the lungs of wisdom bearer and surrounds his/her every step.

Take out a clock or watch with a second hand for this exercise. Take an inhalation breath for 10 seconds, then hold it for 10 seconds. Take a fuller breath and hold it for a longer time. And finally, take an inhalation breath, sucking in small amounts beyond the earlier capacity and hold your breath as long as you are able. Feel free to release the breath with a hardy sound. Notice your feelings and sensations from expanding your limits, taking in more and possibly bridging to something greater.

This time, try focusing your attention on opening each chakra with a long inhalation. Start by moving downward from the crown chakra over the head. Long breath in and connect. Second third eye, long breath in, feel the connection. Third, over your throat, long breath in, opening your expression. Fourth, over your heart, long breath in, expand your ability to be unconditional. Fifth, breath in under your solar plexus, activate your power. Sixth above your genitals, breath in, awaken your creative erotic self. And finally, breathe in opening your base chakra at the perineum feeling grounded to survive.

The Elder is clear to ground him/herself raising the attention to the heavens and gathering the energies of the air to touch the earth.

Notice any feelings or sensations from this exercise.

If your skin is wrinkled, try this exercise. (If you do not have any noticeable wrinkles, find a scar or blemish to focus on.) Using the essential oils suggested in this section, or creating an ointment to put on your wrinkles, scar or blemish, celebrate these areas. What stories do these wrinkles, scars or blemishes have to tell you? Allow yourself to use breath to awaken these areas of your body and to feel their messages. Write down or record somehow what you learned as you anointed, breathed and honored these areas of your body and the stories they represent. Follow this exercise to the next step and share this wisdom, awareness or story with another person. The Elder teaches what he knows. Teach what you've learned.

Thank the air for supporting you.

Mystic

Looking into a mirror in your imagination (mind's eye) affirm these statements:

Half Moon Pose
Ardha Chandrasana

I am a (queer) mystic

I am one with the universe.

I am one with myself.

I am free from separateness that does not serve my highest good.

I am part of the flow.

I can create all possibilities and expressions of love.

I am willing to appear foolish

Finally imagine what you would be like if you could transform your need for approval and acceptance to celebrate what might appear to others as foolishness. Also imagine what you would be like if the illusion of separateness was no longer useful.

Take a moment to activate and seal your affirmation as a Mystic by anointing yourself on each chakra with a mixture of rose (awakening the highest passion) and pine (grounding heaven to earth). You might use these after bathing in the morning, to start your day or before sleep time to empower your dream states. Both are excellent times to absorb the vibration of the plant/essence oil.

The Mystic is radiant with Divine Love. Light/Gold is the element of the mystical life. Passion for the Beloved is the uniting force of creating this radiance. In a fully darkened room or on the land during the new moon, get naked. In the dark, awaken your body with full belly breaths while beginning to caress and stimulate your body. Allow yourself to dance with movements of perfect freedom. Introduce sounds that you might express in making love. Continue to play with yourself, flowing with breath and movement as if you were Sufi dancing. Imagine delicious moments you have had caressing, kissing, making love to partners, knowing each one have been the face of God. Now lay down for a moment, let the image of light within you grow and expand from your heart center out through all parts of your body. See your energy field as light in this darkened space. Notice if the space seems somehow brighter even while dark. Close this experience with one hand at your crown and one hand at your base. Affirm to yourself, "I am one with the essence of all of creation. I am one."

The Mystic knows the sacredness of all things and that all things are an expression of Source. Gold, the element and color of radiance and riches will be used in this ritual as an offering for yourself to another. If you live in the U.S., a gold dollar coins can be purchased at a bank. (In other countries, you might find other gold-plated coins of differing values.)

In a private space, again such as a room with bright daylight or on the land in the sunlight, hold your gold coin with one hand or place it on your body throughout the ritual. As in other exercises, begin to pleasure yourself while holding the coin. Imagine the healing light of the sun and the energetic light from within you charging the gold coin. Spend as much time in this ritual as you desire. Notice your relationship to this coin. The Divine Source is much like our relationship to our resources. How does it feel to bring this gold coin and pleasure together? Affirm to yourself, "I receive abundance and I give abundance freely." After you have journaled your awarenesses, finish this exercise at some future moment by giving this gold coin to someone. Notice then how that feels.

Thank the light for supporting you.

Prophet

Looking into a mirror or in your imagination (mind's eye) affirm these statements:

Tree Pose
Vrksasana

I am a (queer) prophet.

I am a messenger of_____

(What comes to your mind or knowing?)

I have a mission to_____

I have a voice.

I can trust myself and the Divine to speak through me.

I am willing to take risks.

I am willing to follow my guidance (rational, intuitive, heart, body and vision)

I have the power to influence change.

I am willing to be wrong in the judgment of others to follow my truth.

Finally, imagine what you would be like if you could transform the unnecessary caution you may have to follow your heart's desires.

Take a moment to activate/seal your affirmation as a Prophet by anointing yourself on each chakra with a mixture of orange blossom (to integrate one's truth), frankincense (to release all attachments), and mint (to foster healing). You might use these after bathing in the morning, to start your day or before sleep time to empower your dream states. Both are excellent times to absorb the vibration of the essential oil.

This book began of speaking of Queer people by their very nature are prophetic. The Queer Prophet brings a message, a vibration and sound to the orchestra shared by all tribes. These messages of love, inclusion, equality, justice, mercy, abundance, all have a vibration or sound that each of us offer to create our world.

What is your heart sound? Try chanting "om" three times to begin. What do you notice in your body as you chant "om?" Now, explore the vowel sounds or tone repeatedly "a" or "ah,", "e," "i," "o," "oh." Are you aware of any of these tones activating all your energy centers from base to crown?

Again, if you are able to be naked in a room or on the land, try this exercise. Standing in the da Vinci man's pose, breathing in through your heart, send the energy through your body to the earth. Then gather the energy with the next breath from the earth to your heart. Take another breath extending the energy from your heart to the sky. Then with another breath, gather the energy from above down to your heart again.

As a Prophet, you stand naked gathering energy from the earth and sky to open your heart. Finish this exercise by voicing a sound that comes from your heart.

Every Thursday in San Francisco, some Quakers, Buddhists along with people of various religions, lay people and sometimes some Flesh and Spirit brothers sit meditating in front of the Federal Building or hold signs of peace. This has gone on for years now.

The ritual in closing I would encourage might be to use the pleasuring prayer exercise with yourself or a group and then go sit in front of the Federal Building in San Francisco or some place where you wish to offer a peaceful message of support for your community prophetically. What might that be like? The pleasuring prayer exercise also might be used after attending some form of activism as well. Ecstatic work can support all aspects of your life. Transform the world by making it juicier.

Thank sound for supporting you.

Head Stand Pose
Salamba Sirsasana

In conclusion, with this series of exercises and rituals imagine what might take place and what might be manifested if all of Flesh and Spirit Community (or your community of affiliation) could live more fully in the affirmations of the Peaceful Warrior, Lover, Sacred Prostitute, Elder, Mystic and Prophet. What new consciousness might we produce?

Listen to the wisdom of your body
and change the world.

Lovingly, Kirk

IX. Biographical Sketch of the author, his partner and Flesh & Spirit Board & Staff

Dr. Kirk Prine, CMT, is a healer, an integrative bodyworker, teaching Reiki Master, Director of Flesh & Spirit Community, artist, conscious activist and author of *Erotic Body Prayer: Pathways to Pray Through the Body and Build Ecstatic Community*. For seventeen years, Kirk was a psychotherapist directing a counseling center for LGBT people. His work of blending his training in counseling, spirituality and somatic/erotic work has been pioneering and visionary for a new consciousness among the Queer tribe.

Dr. Prine has a B.A. in Theology, with a focus on healing practices across many spiritual traditions; a M.Ed., and Ed.D. in counseling, specializing in behavioral medicine, sexuality and group work; and a CMT with training in Swedish/Esalen massage, Jin Shin Do acupressure, rebirthing, Deep Tissue massage, Amma (a Japanese massage therapy), bodywork for people facing life threatening illness, and sexual healing work as a sacred intimate. Dr. Prine is trained in energy work, emphasizing therapeutic touch, and attuned as a Traditional Reiki Master.

Prior to practicing in the Bay Area, Dr. Prine spent 17 years as a psychotherapist. His practice for queer people specialized in addictions/recovery (family dysfunction, chemical and sexual). Clinically trained as a sex therapist and trauma and grief counselor his work prepared him well for his roles which followed.

During that period he was also the co-director of the Healing and Recovery Workshops, Inc., where he co-facilitated weekly groups on alternative healing and complimentary therapies. For six years he served as adjunct professor at the University of Cincinnati, teaching complimentary therapies as they relate to HIV. Dr. Prine served on the faculty of the East Central AIDS Education and Training Center in Cincinnati, Ohio.

As an integrative bodyworker, Dr. Prine has pioneered new models for erotic spiritual practice. His practice has empowered many queer men to be lovers of their bodies and souls, and to create intentional erotic and spiritual community through body-mind-spirit integration. The call for queer men's community now has developed into the Flesh & Spirit Community. Kirk with his husband Donny Lobree work together in these adventures.

Donny Lobree is a violinist, practitioner of Iyengar Yoga, bodyworker, Reiki channel and student of alchemy. As founder of Healing Notes, a nongovernmental organization, he travels internationally to hospitals and hospices sharing his music with patients as a sound healer. In addition, Donny is a Midwife to the Dying and assists the terminally ill with their "birthing" into death. His first children's book, *How the Waif Bunny Saved the Boy*, will be published shortly.

The Flesh and Spirit Community Board of Directors

Reed Waller, M.A. is Board President. Reed facilitates

ecstatic dance and massage events for the community, practices massage and energy healing, provides computer technical support, and is a management consultant for nonprofit organizations.

Patrick Armstrong, CMT, is an integrative bodyworker and is the Board Vice-President, Volunteer Coordinator and member of the Retreat Planning and Technology Committees. Patrick is a teaching Reiki Master and also facilitates Reiki healing sessions and teaches Peaceful Warrior workshops.

Douglas Smith, M.S. in Counseling, is a Reiki Master and is sensitive to insights into and from the spirit realm. Douglas is the Flesh and Spirit Reiki Coordinator and serves the Board as Secretary.

Bob "Goat" Conrad, B.S., Biology. At an early age he had the privilege of being taken into the woods by family members to learn about the Druid path. Goat is on the Retreat Planning, Finance and Programs Committees.

Skip McDonough has a long history of working with AIDS related nonprofits in the Washington, DC area. He serves on the Board as Treasurer and is our Fundraising Coordinator. He also serves on the Finance Committee.

Gary Ost is an out parish priest in the Episcopal Church with additional responsibilities assisting the LGBTQ work of his diocese. Gary works on the Retreat Planning and Programs Committees.

Bob Russell holds a B.S. in Electrical Engineering and works in the computer industry. Bob is on the Technology and Retreat Planning Committees.

Michael J. Guimon, M.Ed, is a priest and has ministered as a chaplain and guidance counselor in urban schools across the U.S. Michael is on the Newcomers Committee and is a Community Building Night facilitator.

Bill Essex, B.A. Sociology, is trained in Core Shamanic and JourneyWork Techniques and is a teaching Reiki Master. He is the Flesh and Spirit Promotion Coordinator, and an Energy Medicine and Peaceful Warrior workshop facilitator.

Flesh & Spirit Facilitative Staff

Steve Marlowe is a healer, teaching Reiki master, and Peaceful Warrior teacher. He has been planning and facilitating workshops and retreats for queer men on spiritual paths since 1991 including retreats for several Metropolitan Community Churches, Gay Men's Spiritual Retreat, and the Flesh & Spirit Community.

Don Clark, Ph.D., is the author of the ground-breaking book *Loving Someone Gay* and the forthcoming memoir, *Becoming Someone Gay*. For many years Don Clark has been a therapist and guide to gay men. He is a mentor to Kirk Prine and an elder to the Flesh & Spirit Community. (www.donclarkphd.com)

Brandon Maruca is a teaching Reiki Master and team

facilitator of our Peaceful Warrior workshops.

Rev. Dan Newman, Ph.D.,D.D., is a holistic health consultant, Native American spirituality practitioner, artist, safer sex educator and holistic workshop facilitator. Dan has been assisting in Flesh & Spirit work since its inception. (www.ceucert.com)

Jim Stratton, M.A., is a counselor with expertise in recovery areas of addictions, HIV concerns, abuse and sexual healing. Jim has assisted in Flesh & Spirit workshops and retreats since it's beginning.

Allen Siewert, CMT, is a Sacred Intimate in San Francisco. For the past 6 years he has been introducing men all over the country to conscious BDSM play as a staff member of the Power Surrender and Intimacy workshops. He is the web designer for Flesh & Spirit's web site and facilitates ecstatic flogging workshops for Flesh & Spirit Community. (www.allensi.com)

Terry Huwe, M.L.I.S., is a Reiki Practitioner, co-author of the first edition of the Erotic Body Prayer Manual and has been a facilitator of the Flesh and Spirit workshop series.

Ed Kitchen, CMT, is a massage therapist, Reiki Master and has facilitated Flesh and Spirit workshops and retreats.

Ed Wyre has been walking in beauty for more than a decade first by facilitating GaySpirit Drum Circles and now as a Flesh and Spirit Monthly Drum Circle facilitator.

Michael Knotz II is a certified yoga instructor in the Viniyoga tradition and has facilitated yoga for the Flesh & Spirit Community.

Vin Constabileo is one of our drumming circle facilitators.

Guest Facilitators:

Dave Nimmons, is the founder of Manifest Love a national movement helping Gay men envision and create a more humane and affectionate Gay culture. Dave also facilitates retreats with the Flesh & Spirit Community. (www.manifestlove.org)

John Ballew, M.S., is a licensed professional counselor and a massage therapist in private practice in Atlanta. He has facilitated retreats for the Flesh & Spirit Community. (www.bodymindsoul.org)

John Stasio is teacher for the *Erotic Body Prayer* Retreat at Saratoga Springs, CA. John is a founder of the Easton Mountain Retreat Center, and of its resident spiritual community of men who love men. He is also a spiritual teacher, an international retreat/workshop facilitator, a therapist/coach, social justice activist and a writer. (www.stasio.com)

Ann McGinnis, CMT, is a movement therapist and facilitates Flesh & Spirit's *The Mystic* workshop held for men and women together.

Notes, Sources, and Image Credits

Preface
1. Frederick C. Mesh, et al., *Webster's Ninth New Collegiate Dictionary* (Springfield, MA: Merriam-Webster Incorporated, 1984)
2. JeanHouston, *Jump Time: Shaping Your Future in a World of Radical Change*
Photo p. 5, Allen Siewert, Flesh & Spirit logo with phoenix
Photo p. 6, Allen Siewert, Photograph of 981 Haight immediately after fire.
3. Neil Douglas-Klotz, *Prayers of the Cosmos: Meditations on the Aramaic Words of Jesus* (thanks to Rev. Dr Penny Nixon for this reference, from one of her sermons)
4. Flesh & Spirit Community, Mission/Visioning Statement
Photo p. 13, Allen Siewert, Flesh & Spirit *Ecstatic Gatekeepers Retreat*

Chapter I
Loving Ideas: Political and Spiritual Archetypes
1. Solomon, *Revised Standard Bible*, Ecclesiastes 1:9
2. Alice Walker, *Anything We Love Can Be Saved*

Chapter II
Erotic Body Prayer: The Journey of Healing
1. Matthew Simmons, presentation to International Conference on Prostitution, Los Angeles, CA, ASSECT and UCLA sponsored.

2. Lester B. Brown, *Two Spirit People: American Indian Lesbian Women and Gay Men*

3. Tommi Avicolli Mecca, "Humanity's true heroes: Stephen Funk is being court-martialed, and we should be angry about it." *San Francisco Bay Guardian,* July 23, 2003

4. Long Term Survivors Studies: Michael Callen, *Surviving and Thriving with AIDS*; George Solomon, "Psychoneuro-immunology and AIDS: Characteristics;" George Solomon, "Psychoneuroimmunology: Interactions between the Central Nervous System and the Immune System," *Journal of Neuroscience Research*, 1987:18:1-9; K. Pelletier, D. Herzing, "Psychoneuroimmmunology: Toward a mind-body model," *Advances*, 1989:5; R. Adler, *Pyschoneuroimmunology* (New York, NY: Academic Press, 1991); Robert Remien, "Long-term survivors of AIDS;" S.C. Kobassa, et al. "Type A and Hardiness," *Journal of Behavioral Medicine*, Vol 6, 1983; S.C. Kobassa, "Personality and resistance to Illness," *American Journal of Community Psychology* (1979); John P. Capitanio, Sally P. Mendoza, Nicholas W. Lerche, and William A. Mason "Social stress results in altered glucocorticoid regulation and shorter survival in simian acquired immune deficiency syndrome;" N.C. Lovejoy, R. Sisson "Psychoneuroimmunology and AIDS," *Holistic Nurse Practitioner* (1989); Carl Simonton, Greg Anderson, *Cancer: 50 Essential Things to Do*, Bernie Siegel, *A Hope and a Prayer* (video); Deepak Chopra, *Spontaneous Healing.*

5. Kirk Prine, Sue Taft, Marilyn Gugel, "A Healing Journey for the HIV Challenged Person."

Diagram p. 27, Kirk Prine.

6. Victor Frankel, *Man's Search for Meaning.*

7. Charles Whitfield, *Healing the Child Within: Characteristics of Safe and Unsafe People.*

8. Marianne Williamson, *Return to Love*, "Our Greatest Fear." Moving from Victim to Survivor

9. Wayne Jackson, "The Falwell-Gay Alliance," Soul Force project Nov 8, 1999.

10 Greg Louganis, *Beneath the Surface*, Interview with Barbara Walters.

11. Joseph Carver, *Love and Stockholm Syndrome: The Mystery Of Loving An Abuser.*

12. Jonathan Van Meter, "Anderson Cooper Unanchored" New York Magazine, Sept. 19, 2005.

13. Franklin Abbott, *Fact Sheets on Fathers of Gay Men*

14. Jalal ad-Din Muhammad Rumi, trans. Coleman Barks, *Essential Rumi.*

15. Kelly Cogswell, *Gay Pride Jerusalem: Making History in the Holy City.*

16. Jalal ad-Din Muhammad Rumi, trans. Coleman Barks, *Essential Rumi.*

17. Nancy Qualls-Corbett, *The Sacred Prostitute: Eternal Aspect of the Feminine*, pp. 22-3.

18. James M. Robinson, ed., selection from *The Nag Hammadi Library*, revised edition (Harper Collins: San Francisco, 1990.

19. Population Resource Center projections from 2000-2050

20. Burt H. Hoff, Interview with Malidoma Patrice Somé, "Gays: Guardians of the Gates."

21. Don Clark, *Loving Someone Gay.*
Photo of Don Clark, p. 46, Geo Gaile, permission of Don Clark, caption quote from *Ecstatic Gatekeepers* retreat.

22. Somé, Malidoma Patrice, workshop on Ancestor Wisdom,

Learning Annex, San Francisco, 2001.

Walt Whitman image p. 47 courtesy of the Library of Congress, LC-DIG-ppmsca-07142, partial image. Engraved frontispiece by Samuel Hollyer from first edition *Leaves of Grass*, 1865.

23. Mother Teresa of Calcutta, public talk on Love, St. Peter and Chains, Cincinnati, 1997.

24. G. Hirsch, Frederick McCurdy, Joseph Jacobs, *Prophets and Prophecy.*

25. Thomas Huxley, quoted by Harry Hay, Creating Change Conference, Oakland CA, 1998.

26. Shimakataya.

p. 60, Photograph of Rev. Elder Jim Mitulski courtesy of Metropolitan Community Church of San Francisco Archives.

27. Mattie Stepanek, "On Growing Up (Part 5)."

28. Rowena Pantaleon, "Kontomble Merging Mentoring Program."

29. Gary Drake, conversation with Kirk Prine.

Chapter III
Kirk's Personal Journey

1. Kirk Prine et al., "A Healing Journey for the HIV Challenged Person."

2. Rumi, trans. Barks, *Essential Rumi.*

Chapter IV
Erotic Body Prayer

1. Sri Ronji (Ron Roth), *Prayer and the Five Stages of Healing*

2. Sri Ronji (Ron Roth), 5-day intensive, San Diego, 2001

3. Larry Dossey, Healing Words: *The Power Of Prayer and the*

Practice of Medicine.

4. Elizabeth Kübler-Ross, Public Lecture on "Healing Possibilities," AIDS Living in Recovery Conference, Cincinnati, Ohio, 199

Page 86, Charcoal drawing by Dan Newman

George Solomon, *Psychoneuroimmunology.*

6. Candace B. Pert, "Emotions and Healing," Public talk at Healing Circle of Cincinnati, 1991, and *Molecules of Emotion* 1999.

7. Deepak Chopra, *Quantum Healing: Exploring the Frontiers of Mind/Body Medicine,* 1989.

Chapter V
Healing Stories and Therapeutic Practice

1. Deepak Chopra, *The Gift of Love* (Audio CD readings from Rumi).

Page 92, photograph of Matt Johnson, 2006, by Rich Stadtmiller, www.RichTrove.com.

Chapter VI
Simple Steps For Erotic Body Prayer

Page 100, photograph of crop circles by Steve and Karen Alexander.

1. Shankari the Alchemist, Shankari Retreat Center Bali, Indonesia. www.Shankari.com

2. Louise Hay, public talk, AIDS, Medicine and Miracles Conference.

3. *Bible,* American Standard Version, I Cor 6:19

4. Louie Nassaney, Healing Alternatives Conference, Los Angeles, CA.

Page 110, Chakra image by Allen Siewert, based on Kirk Prine model of survivor attributes.

Pages 120 & 122, screen images from Flesh & Spirit intake interview video.

5. Morihei Ueshiba, quotations compiled by O-Sensei (stated in Introduction by John Stevens for *Aikido*)

Pages 207-8, Reiki Symbols by Kirk Prine, received from Nancy Lard, TRM (additional reference Donna Stein, Essential Reiki)

6. Elizabeth Clare Prophet, *Violet Flame to Heal Body, Mind and Soul.*

7. Joseph Kramer, *Fire on the Mountain-Male Genital Massage* (DVD).

Page 131, John and Company, photographs of Sculpture and Wood carving of Lingam. www.MuddsArt.com

Page 132, Willendorf Goddess replica image (from 30,000-20,000 BC).

Page 137, photograph by Allen Siewert, Kirk Prine modeling Big Draw.

Pages 139 & 140, photographs by Vince Gabrielly (www.raven-gallery.com)

8. Michael Winkelman, "The Therapeutic Effects of Drumming: Group Drumming Boost Cancer-Killer Cells," *American Journal of Public Health*, April 2003, Vol. 93, Issue 4, pp. 647-53; Michael Winkelman, "Drumming Out Addiction."

Pages 144-5, photographs by Bill Essex of Kirk Prine and Donny Lobree at their pre-wedding henna ritual.

Page 146, photograph by Donny Lobree of Curt Keyer.

9. Email from Curt Keyer.

10. Annette Goodheart, "HealingLaughter" AIDS Living in

Recovery Conference, Cincinnati, Ohio, 1990.

Page 149, Flesh And Spirit photo of the Friend (the Ancestors) being carried and dropped.

11. Veronica Franco, as portrayed in the film *Dangerous Beauty* (screenplay by Jeannine Dominy, derived from the book *The Honest Courtesan: Veronica Franco, Citizen and Writer in Sixteenth Century* by Margaret F. Rosenthal)

12. *Bible*, American Standard Version, James 5:16

13. Rumi, trans. by Barks, *Essential Rumi*

Chapter VII
Postscript: A Developing Community

1. William Shultz, *Group Dynamics*, 1966.

2. Carter Heyward, quoted at MCC-SF.

3. Harvey Milk, quoted by Randy Shilts, *The Mayor of Castro Street The Life and Times of Harvey Milk.* p. 363

Page 169, Bob (Goat) Conrad, photograph of tree rings.

Page 172, Leadership Development Model by Kirk Prine

Chapter VIII
Archetype Exercises and Rituals and Yoga Asanas

Pages 176-92, photographs by Allen Siewert of Donny Lobree demonstrating Aikido exercises and yoga poses.

Additional Reference: J.A. Wiley, "Comparison of alcohol and drug use patterns of homosexual and heterosexual men: the San Francisco Men's Health Study." *Drug Alcohol Depend* 1988(Oct);22(1-2):63-73.

Upcoming in 2007

Flesh & Spirit Community

Erotic Body Prayer in Bali Indonesia

An International Retreat for Queer Men on a Spiritual Journey

March 8-13, 2007, in Bali, Indonesia

Erotic Body Prayer Retreat

May 3 - 6, 2007

Saratoga Springs, California

For more information visit:
www.fleshandspirit.org